I0712003

# WHAT MAKES DOLPHINS LAUGH:
## The Story of 'Boy'

### By Robert F. Burgess

**Spyglass Publications**
308 W. Marion Street
Chattahoochee, Florida 32324

According to a
dolphin named
Boy
**We Do!**

# WHAT MAKES DOLPHINS LAUGH:
## The Story of 'Boy'
## By Robert F. Burgess

**SPYGLASS PUBLICATIONS, CHATTAHOOCHEE, FLORIDA**



A 2020 Paperback Edition
For information address:

Robert F. Burgess
Spyglass Publications
308 West Marion Street
Chattahoochee, Florida 32324

Laughing Dolphin Photograph
Courtesy Wikipedia Images
Cover Design Robert F. Burgess

Author photo by Charles Harnage Jr.

*This book is warmly dedicated
To dolphin lovers everywhere*

# TABLE OF CONTENTS

## CHAPTER 1

# Close Encounters of the Fourth Kind

I was entering another world, one full of dangerous aliens far different than the one in which I lived. It was an airless world that had not entirely been explored. My companion hovering weightless above me stared down through his glass window watching me descend into the unknown, watching me but unable to give me any help if I needed it. I was without a weapon and came bearing gifts of food for any of the aliens who might confront me. My only solace was the ancient encrusted statue 25-feet below me of Jesus Christ who stood 9-feet tall. Yes, this was evidence that Man had been here before. Maybe if I landed near him the aliens would go easier on me.

How wrong I was.

The strange new world I had entered had never been totally explored by Man. But the part I was in had been. That was why the trouble began.

Two incredibly large alien inhabitants were immediately in my face and I had not even reached Jesus yet! I wore thin red and white gloves so I motioned scram toward the closest one since he was gnashing his teeth in my face.

Apparently accustomed to our sign language he got my message and turned away. The other creature wasn't that close to me but his face was hideous. Bulging green eyes the size of golf balls, a slobbering mouth that hung open and drooled. A head the size of garbage can lid.

With my other gloved hand I made the same threatening

wave and by golly he lunged forward and struck me! I instantly balled my fist and punched his ugly mug.

We both fell back in surprise. I was shocked by this sudden attack. I looked up at my staring buddy whose eyes were almost as large as the alien's. All he did was shrug. Big help he was!

This less than peaceful encounter began a few miles off the coast of Florida's Key Largo. I was peacefully sinking down beside Italy's gift to us of their Christ of the Abyss statue in 25-feet of water when these two bozos waylaid me almost as soon as I got underwater.

Usually I never carry food with me but in this case I had a Gaines-Burger in one pocket and a chicken leg in the other. I planned to do some close-up photography of fish eating out of my hand. Being a novice at this I was about to get my first lesson in what not to do in this endeavor.

The first big guy that stuck his face in mine was a six-foot long barracuda as big around as a telephone pole with a rack of sharp ivories he kept clicking at me.

The other over-sized thug that attacked me was a dark brown Goliath Grouper magnified in the water to the size of a small Volkswagen.

His mouth looked wider than my shoulders and it hung open like he was drooling all over the place. Camera in right hand at eye level, strobe in my left hand held high, I slowly advanced on this alien from another world. Since my ultra-wide angle lens could get an entire diver on film when I was three feet from him I moved in close to my drooling friend. I saw one of his bulging green eyes roll up and look at my strobe above him and the other rolled down looking at my swim fins below him. He didn't back up an inch. He just kept staring and drooling. I thought, what the heck does he want? Both of these guys were right on me as soon as I got in the water. Then I thought someone must feed them here. If so they expected…no, they demanded…that I give them a handout. Those who know call that a 'Conditioned Reflex."

The animal has been trained to perform, so now he is given a reward. When he gets no reward, he gets angry and does threatening things like clicking his teeth and biting people. Who is to blame for this behavior? People like me, of course.

As I snapped pictures of this big guy we both were slowly sinking into deeper water beside the statue. I knew my photos would be useless. No one could see the size of this brute because they had nothing to compare it to. Not only that but I realized as I looked at him that he was watching the white sand bottom coming up to meet us and he was slowly changing color to match it, changing from dark brown to dirty white. At the same time I thought, if he wants a handout I'll give him half of my dog's hamburger, the plastic-wrapped Gaines- Burger in the right pocket of my Buoyancy Compensator vest.

When we got to the bottom I put the camera and strobe under my left arm and with my right I went into the pocket for the Gaines- Burger.

As I slowly drew it out I carefully unwrapped it. My friend with the bulging eyes was immediately interested. He drew closer now. He knew he was going to get fed. His big green eyes really bulged now and his slack jaws looked to be slobbering more than ever. I started to hand him the dog burger and again he lunged forward to get it. I let it go fast and jerked back my hand as he gulped, then blew the empty wrapper back at me!

He apparently liked the dog food. Now he looked like he wanted the main course. Well, I wasn't going to give it to him. I clutched my camera and took off. He followed me over two reefs before I finally lost him.

I ended up in a pleasant little valley with amber walls of coral on each side. It was a pretty place. A peaceful school of 8-inch long yellow snappers slowly swam around in the middle.

At last, here were my peaceful fish that I could feed quietly from my left hand while I shot close-ups of them nibbling the chicken leg.

I took it out of my BC pocket about to unwrap it when **BLAM! It was gone!**

The school of yellow snappers raced around me chasing one of their members that had the end of the chicken leg sticking out of his mouth!

That was the last time I tried to feed fish.


Back at Key Largo's Pennecamp Coral Reef State Park I told park ranger Mark Yelvington about my encounter. I hardly began when he said,

"I bet you were at the Christ of the Abyss Statue."

"Yeah, how did you know?"

Mark grinned. "That's where a dive master from one of the dive shops always feeds that big barracuda there. He puts a fish in his teeth and the cuda flashes by and cuts it off just shy of his nose for the video cameraman. So far he still has his nose."

I just shook my head.


The next day Mark joined me at the Christ of the Abyss statue where the big grouper was still waiting and slobbering. I finally snapped the photograph I wanted. Mark got that big fellow to pose by offering him his yellow dive glove. I shot a side view so readers could see the size of the grouper compared to Mark. Whenever that picture appeared in a magazine it was usually a two-page spread with the giant Goliath on one page and across the seam on the opposite page was Mark. The grouper was almost the same size as the diver!


We sailed back to our mooring in Key Largo Sound; then took our tanks ashore for air fills. Walking around Key Largo that afternoon I came to a large fenced in area where you could pay $10 to swim with the dolphins. It was such a novel idea I thought it would make a fun feature for one of the Sunday weeklies. I asked the manager/owner if he minded me photographing the action. He said he would be glad to have me do it.

So I shot pictures of the arriving guests and the eagerly watching dolphins. They looked like a bunch of loud, disorderly teenage guys to me. Not a female amongst them. No wonder they were so rowdy.

After I took the topside photos I asked the owner if he minded me shooting some underwater shots. He said it was fine. I grabbed my mask and fins out of my truck, slung the Nikonos V over my shoulder and I was ready.

Later I interviewed the owner for a feature. He told me that during the winter months he toured with the dolphins and during the off-season he let them burn off pent-up energy playing with people who paid to join the fun. Each group going into the pool with the dolphins were given a briefing on what to expect and how to play with these energetic fellows. While they were giving this introduction I noticed all the dolphins lined up with glittering eyes watching for the fun to begin. Again I got the impression of teenaged boys checking out the prettiest cheerleaders at their home football game.

As the guests slowly trooped into the water to join the dolphins it was pandemonium in the pool. Everyone began splashing and, yelling; the dolphins yap-yap-yapping as they cavorted with the people, their big glistening gray bodies torpedoing in and around, then over and around, under, back and forth, never hitting a single person but having the time of their lives along with everyone else. They raced around the visitors, and pushed each other as though competing for someone to play with.

It was fascinating. They were just like eager kids checking out the new arrivals. And interestingly, most of the new arrivals were just that – eager teenagers with a few Grandmas thrown in.

Before long they were all paired up at the other end of the pool where the people held onto dorsal fins as the dolphins sped back and forth towing the screaming visitors around the pool.

This went on for a period of time and everyone obviously enjoyed the interspecies experience, especially the energetic dolphins. They laughed and squawked above water and peppered everyone with high-pitched clicks as they inspected everyone inside and out, and then seemed to discuss it with one another. After a while I slid into the water with them.

Underwater there seemed to be more pandemonium that on top. These were all male dolphins and they almost looked as though they were vying for different girls to choose them for the fast tow trips. When one dolphin seemed to have his mate picked out, another larger male might bump him aside and take his place.

Later I asked the owner what they were doing. They seemed to be fighting over which of the girls were more attractive. He shrugged and said, "I don't know. Sometimes they fight over a guy."

I was glad they paid me no attention because these were big bull dolphins. They raced around me as though I wasn't even there. They ignored me but they were clicking so vigorously it seemed they were all talking at once. They hurled themselves around the pool seeming to squabble about who they were to take for a ride but not one of them even brushed me.

It reminded me of a time when I was exploring an underground cave near my home in north Florida. I had just crawled down a narrow tunnel and could stand and squeeze through a narrow vertical crack into a larger room where I had been before. My light showed it to be a large domed rock room with a pool of water below me in its middle. A 2-foot wide rock ledge encircled the pool 10 feet below. The entire ceiling of the chamber was covered with hanging bats. When I squeezed through that crack every bat in that room decided to make a panic exit to get out of the cave as I came in. Every bat there went through that crack about the same time I did and not a one touched me. The dolphins used the same kind of sonar the bats did to avoid me. At that moment my buddy snapped a picture of me with the bats. Hard to believe because they were all around me. Same in the pool with the dolphins.

When our gang left the pool these fun-loving fellows really seemed disappointed to see us go. As a new batch of guests arrived and the briefing began, the dolphins were all standing on their heads waving their tails goodbye to the departing people. What a great bunch of performers!

Looking at prices today to swim or meditate with a dolphin, the charge is usually at least three figures. Check on-line for prices. The current charge for a dolphin encounter on Key Largo is $165 for an adult or a child (10 years +). An adult observer is charged $39.95.

Understandably, I guess, today it has become a lucrative business, thanks to the mystique surrounding such encounters. Being with a dolphin for a separate "treatment" is believed by some to be a very special experience. Especially for the afflicted. Others however, including some in the medical profession feel that the effects are only temporary on a par with meeting a family pet. Why and how such things happen is unknown. That's the nature of these "Close Encounters of the Third Kind." For those who believe and pay to play it is all relative. Who knows? Miracles do happen.

## CHAPTER 2

# Something Different Out There

My dive buddy, Doug Bogert, and I were enjoying DEMA's (Diving Equipment & Marketing Association's) conference in New Orleans one year when we saw an unusual dive film. It was about Robert Marx and his crew searching for the wreck of *Nuestra Señora de las Maravillas,* a Spanish treasure galleon lost in the far reaches of the Little Bahamas Bank in 1656.

Marx found part of the wreck and it was a good documentary but what intrigued me more was a brief film they had shot of Marx's wife, Jennifer free-diving with a pod of thirty dolphins that visited them every day. We have all seen these kinds of videos where the dolphins relate to divers. But this one was somehow different because the dolphins seemed to be overly responsive to Jennifer. They welcomed her like a long lost cousin.

They crowded around her like children eager to please her; like pets begging to be petted. When I saw Marx and mentioned this he told me he could almost set his watch to the pod appearing for their play period with his wife each day. He said they seemed really hungry for attention.

I wrote it off to the fact that Marx and his salvage team were out in limbo, so far from the usual boating activity in the Bahamas that these mammals might be starved for attention. It was obvious from their daily appearance around the treasure hunters that they hugely enjoyed being with the divers working in their playground.

That thought reminded me of the time my fishing buddy, Dr. Jim Thomson, and I purposely took his boat far out into a seldom-fished area of the Gulf of Mexico called The Middle Ground because it was so far offshore. We ran slowly trolling for fish. As we did, two dolphins swam up and one of them stayed at our bow riding our bow wave. I moved forward, lay down and reached over and ran my hand down his back. Jim slowed the boat and the two dolphins appeared beside us. The one I had touched swam back and forth beside us as though inviting me to get in the water with him. I waved to him and he nodded and seemed to be talking. He reminded me of a dog with a stick begging me to throw it so he could go get it. I told Jim that there was no doubt at all that if I got in the water with that dolphin we would have us a good time playing together. It was quite a temptation.

One other tale needs telling because it seemed so unreal, yet it happened exactly as I am telling it. I have a 16-foot live-aboard ComPac sailboat that I trailer to the Gulf Coast or to the Florida Keys to dive for lobsters. On one trip to the Gulf Coast I had Bob Sofge our Methodist minister aboard. Bob and I were scuba diving buddies. It was late afternoon and we were sailing toward our overnight anchorage behind the barrier island of the bay.

I saw a dolphin jump across the bay. So I told Bob about how all the dolphins in the area used to look forward to sundown boaters coming out in the late afternoon to feed at the ship channel into the bay. The dolphins would come up beside the boats and people threw them snacks.

That went on for some years and then it stopped because the local authorities were afraid the practice would get the dolphins habituated to these handouts rather than their own natural feeding habits. Dolphin lovers were unhappy about this and so were the dolphins. But it did make sense.

But as I was telling the preacher this story over his shoulder I saw that dolphin racing toward our boat. I knew he was going to hit us up for a handout but I didn't know how creative he would be in the process. His timing was perfect because I said to my preacher friend:

"Yup, this time of day they would come looking for their handouts…" and as I said that I gestured with my arm over the side of the boat, just as that big dolphin jumped straight up out of the water right beside us to get whatever I might be offering him.

My heart almost stopped!

The preacher's eyes popped wide open.

Without changing my expression I said, "Like that!" And we sailed on.


In those years I wrote regularly for all of our outdoors magazines. Often I joined Dan Wagner and his group of divers aboard his *Impossible Dream* from south Florida to spend several days diving the far reaches of the Bahamas Islands. When the *Dream* ran into a channel marker and sank I was there aboard one of Blackbeard's sailboats full of divers watching it being salvaged. After that Dan launched the *Dream Too* and we continued our research in the waters of the "deadly" Bermuda Triangle, making dive trips there every few weeks as I gathered new material and photographs for the book I was contracted to write for Tony Bliss of Aqua Quest Publications. As part of their diving series it was published in 1998 titled, *Diving Off The Beaten Track by Bob Burgess.*

I know, but someone had to do it.

That's why six months after seeing Marx's film of the friendly dolphins I found myself aboard the *Impossible Dream* cruising slowly along those golden sand flats scanning the calm waters for that very pod of dolphins.

First we found Marx's crew working part of the wreck of the *Maravillas* and a few of us snorkeled over to see their operation. Then we spent the next couple hours slow-cruising the Bahamas Bank skimming through the calm shallow aqua-green seas so smoothly it enabled us to easily scan the distant bright golden flats with our Polaroid sun glasses. We didn't have to look long to find them.

Or it didn't take them long to find us, which was more likely the case out in those long lonely sand flats where the only possible interest for a school of dolphins would be a shipwreck or a bunch of wayward divers looking for a shipwreck. In this case everyone was glad to find each other in that long lonely outpost.

We saw them coming long before they reached us. It was like watching a growing tsunami of thirty golden-hued dolphins plunging in and out of the water racing toward us at high speed, their glistening arcing bodies in and out of the water glittering bright in the intense Bahamian sun beating down on us. Wave after wave of golden dolphins. There they were the *Maravillas* (Marvelous) Dolphins!

We swiftly stopped, and launched a large outboard-powered inflatable of eager divers. Once the load of divers and the waves of dolphins came together we all met underwater and took stock of each other.

Eager as they were, the dolphins and divers looked at each other but were apprehensive about touching. What surprised me was how big they were. Especially magnified by the water. They moved fast and would come upright looking you directly in your eyes while peppering you with a barrage of whistles and clicks, so rapid they almost flowed together always changing pitches. You couldn't feel it but the dolphins were looking at us inside and out. The dolphin in front of me was looking me over with bright shiny eyes while clicking up a storm. In seconds he knew more about me than I knew myself. I would reach out my gloved hand in greeting but he always stayed just out of reach. But seeing all those smiling faces and curious eyes left the feeling that they were very glad to see us. The feeling of that very special thing was very strong there. They were not only smiling at us, they were mouth-open yap-yap-yapping at us saying in their language maybe how much they liked us being with them. I understood at once what Dr. Lilly meant by that weird feeling you have in those circumstances. You feel you are with very close friends and you want more than anything to embrace them and to tell them how much you appreciate them. Somehow, as we all met, those words and sentiment all got spoken. We may not have understood each other but in their eyes you saw their sentiments and you knew the words were tumbling out. We all felt it and though we could not speak it, we knew they knew and we didn't need to know the words for it. We all felt the emotion. And that was enough.

I swam back to our dive boat to shoot pictures from above and by the time I got the camera the dolphins were all in hot pursuit of the inflatable that raced around us trailed furiously by pursuing dolphins.

Once the excitement subsided the divers climbed back aboard the *Dream Too* and we continued to our next dive site. The dolphins accompanied us riding our bow wave for a while; then peeled off as a group to wherever dolphins go on that great Bahamas Bank.

It pleased me greatly when I returned to find them, or their offspring still there spreading joy *ten years later*.

# CHAPTER 3

# Dolphins in the Mists

Pliny the Younger (A.D. 62-113) wrote, "I have met with a story, which, although authenticated by undoubted evidence, looks very like fable…. There is in Africa a town called Hippo, situated not far from the seacoast; it stands upon a navigable lake, communicating with an estuary in the form of a river, which alternately flows into the lake or into the ocean, according to the ebb and flow of the tide…. " The Roman author then went on to say that people of all ages enjoyed fishing, sailing, and swimming there, and one day, while swimming toward the opposite shore, a youngster met a dolphin which played around him and eventually allowed the boy to ride upon his back.

"The fame of this remarkable accident spread through the town, and crowds of people flocked around the boy…. The next day the shore was thronged with spectators, all attentively watching the ocean and the lake…. The dolphin appeared again and came to the boy, who together with his companions, swam away with the utmost precipitation. The dolphin as though to invite and call them back, leaped and dived up and down, in a series of circular movements.

"This he continued to do for several days until the people got brave enough to enter the water and began playing with him themselves.

"They ventured, therefore, to advance near, playing with him and calling him to them, while he in return suffered himself to be touched and stroked…. The boy, in particular, who first made the experiment, swam by the side of him, and leaping upon his back, was carried backward and forward in that manner, and thought the dolphin knew him and was fond of him, while he too had grown fond of the dolphin. There seemed, now, indeed, to be no fear on either side, the confidence of the boy and the tameness of the other mutually increasing; the rest of the boys in the meantime surrounding and encouraging their companion...."

Was Pliny's story fact or fable? Would wild dolphins, on their own accord, really make friends and play with humans? From a few rare incidences of a remarkably similar nature, we now know that Pliny the Roman was most likely writing the truth.

Apparently, the only thing wild dolphins want from man is companionship. Dolphins in captivity perform for food rewards. But, in instances such as the one described by Pliny the Younger, when dolphins were offered food from the hands of their admirers it was always refused. The dolphins chose to catch their own live fish from the sea. Evidently, food rewards were not the attraction. These marine mammals had nothing else to gain but the friendly, playful relationship itself.

While long-term relationships between wild dolphins and divers in the open ocean are rare, there are at least a dozen incidents a year throughout the world that could be termed something more than mere chance meetings. It has happened in all the waters of the world, from the South Pacific to the Caribbean and the Atlantic. Off the coast of England for over three years a twelve-foot-long male bottlenose dolphin developed one of those rare close relationships with local divers. The British divers found this dolphin, whom they named Donald, caused such a stir with his friendly personality and playful antics that an organization called The International Dolphin Watch was established in the hope of documenting other such encounters throughout the world.

Man has always been fond of his domesticated animals. We make pets of the dog, the cat, even an occasional animal from the wild. We enjoy these animals on a certain level. A special bond develops between man and animal, whether the object of our affections is a venerable old tomcat, or in the case of Joy Adamson of *Born Free* fame, an African lion. For man to befriend, train, and relate to a domestic animal is one thing; to accomplish this with a wild animal is quite another. To pursue this feat into the alien world of the sea with one of its creatures takes on even greater significance. Moreover, when there is the possibility that this animal may possess intelligence on a par with our own, then watch out!

The temptation to see us and our human reactions mirrored in these relationships is overwhelming. How easy it is to anthropomorphize our smiling dolphin friends, this remarkable species of marine mammals that not only always appears to be happy, but extremely clever as well. So far, man has capitalized on this cleverness, this penchant for play, for his own amusement with dolphins in captivity. Perhaps now, by looking more closely at the animals under these conditions, we will see other interesting facets of their collective character. Perhaps we will begin to see behind the enigmatic dolphin smile to that indefinable "something" that has long nurtured the ever-growing dolphin mystique. Only then will we be able to understand why some scientists have selected the dolphin as their most logical choice for man's first breakthrough in interspecies communication.

**CHAPTER 4**

Condensed from *Secret Languages of the Sea*
by Robert F. Burgess

# We See They Hear

To understand how the cetaceans, the air-breathing aliens of our underwater world such as whales and dolphins take in what they see you would have to forget what you see but sharpen what you hear. Sight is our primary sense. Hearing is theirs. To be like them what you heard your brain would process those sounds into sound pictures and store them in your brain for future reference. You would recognize other creatures in your world from the sounds they made or by the echoes you get back from the sounds *you made.*

Everything about where you are and who you are and who is with you would all be based on sound. That would be your primary sense. In the dark or if you closed your eyes you would instantly know everything around you as if you saw it with your eyes. But air-breathing animals like whales and dolphins need not see visually because they "see" it all with their sense of sound.

These remarkable marine air-breathers have very strong sound senses able to perform feats that we human animals of "higher" intelligence can only marvel at. Here is a sample: In a swimming pool a blindfolded dolphin is asked to find a target —a half-inch-long vitamin capsule that has been dropped into the water at the other end of the pool without the dolphin knowing it. Without hesitation and without visual aids, the dolphin swims directly to the invisible target.

In another instance, a dolphin is asked to tell the difference between two pieces of metal painted the same color, one a square of copper and the other a square of brass. Always the dolphin easily picks the copper square from the brass square even though both targets look exactly alike.

Even more amazing, a blindfolded dolphin can instantly "see" you in the water with him; he can also tell things about your internal makeup that only a doctor might otherwise determine with an X-ray.

How is it possible for these marine animals to perform such astounding feats? This is one of the questions researcher Kenneth Norris asked himself upon observing how well dolphins in captivity were able to solve such seemingly unsolvable problems.

It was as if the animals were capable of reading the experimenter's mind, as if they possessed some kind of super sense that replaced their sight so that even though blindfolded they could "see" the tiny targets researchers were asking them to identify.

Thanks to the continued efforts of such early researchers as Norris, we now know that dolphins do indeed possess a super sense—a sound sense—that among other things allows them to pinpoint targets through what we now call echolocation. It is the system whales and dolphins use as their sonar (Sound Navigation and Ranging) systems, even when blindfolded.

One of the first, if not the first, to realize that dolphins use some kind of extraordinary sensing system was Arthur McBride, the first curator of Marine Studios in Florida. McBride captured wild dolphins and displayed them to the public there. Normally his catch boats cornered the dolphins in murky canals and bays and netted them. But what surprised McBride was how easily the dolphins were able to avoid his fine-meshed nets. In muddy water with mere inches of visibility, the dolphins often turned away from his nets long before they reached them. Yet they could neither see nor hear the nets. How did they do it, McBride wondered.

Was it possible that they were using a system similar to that used by bats, and were able to send out sound signals that bounced back to them from off the nets? McBride believed that this was the case. He theorized that bubbles forming on the fine mesh of his nets acted like a solid barrier, bouncing the sound signals back in warning to the dolphins.

If this was true, he could surely check his theory. McBride went after the dolphins with a much larger mesh net, and this time he was successful in capturing them.

McBride was not about to reveal his new knowledge to any potential competitors, and his early awareness of dolphin sonar and his method for foiling it were not revealed until many years later, after his death. When researchers William Schevill and Barbara Lawrence were trying to learn more about how dolphins navigated, they found and published McBride's early field notes. Later, working with independent investigator Winthrop Kellogg at Marineland in Florida, the researchers performed test after test with the captive dolphins at that aquarium and subsequently provided the basis for additional understanding about this unique sense.

It took long enough to learn exactly what the mammals were doing that enabled them to perform such marvelous feats of "seeing with sonar." But it was far more difficult for us to determine exactly how the animals did it. What the researchers found was that all the toothed whales and some of the baleen whales use this sound-navigation system. Somehow these animals sounded a powerful click that swept through the water until it encountered an object denser than the water. Then, an echo of that contact bounced back to the dolphin and was instantly processed by the animal. It told him how far away the object was by the interval between the click and the returning echo. In its simplest terms, this was the basic process. But only high-speed repetition of this clicking and interpretation of returning echoes provided the dolphin with the information he sought.

In their experiments, Schevill and Lawrence found that their test animal could repeatedly echolocate a target fish dropped anywhere in its tank in this manner: the dolphin emitted a series of intense sonar clicks of about twenty to thirty per second, almost simultaneously receiving the echo — the reflected wave altered now in character. As the dolphin turned toward the target, emitting more rapid clicks and noting the changes in the returning echoes, these sound wave modulations told it things about the target's size, speed, location, and makeup of the target fish itself. As its clicking continued, and it closed in on the target, the dolphin had a complete readout of the situation, right up to the moment it ate the prey.

Whales too are able to broadcast a beam of sonic signals with their oil-filled dome on their forehead, then pick up the returning signal not only with the same organ, but with a thin oil located in the dolphin's normally out-thrust jaw. Both areas then direct the sound inward through a so-called "acoustic window," a thin, hollow shell of bone covering an oval area in the rear part of the dolphin's jaw near the skull. And from there it is transmitted to the mammal's inner ear.

Using this dome of oil atop his head called a melon, the dolphin can shape and focus sounds they produce. Dolphins can direct one series of echolocating signals forward in an arc normally covering an area measuring ten degrees on each side of a midline down the dolphin's body; it can simultaneously shoot out a probing side beam. To cover a wider range, the dolphin will swing its head, sweeping the projected beam back and forth.

Researchers learned that the fatty tissue in the dolphin's forehead, the melon, was also capable of focusing this sound — literally beaming it out in different directions, the same way you might beam a spotlight into the darkness to illuminate some object. But astonishingly enough, with the dolphin these echolocation patterns were not only broadcast out at a normal ten degree arc from either side of a midline down the animal's head, but the animal also could shape the beam, make it broader or narrower, or even project a second beam at an angle to the first.

For wide coverage the mammal had only to swing its head from side to side. Moreover, the beam could be fine-tuned. A high-pitched note made up of shortly spaced high-frequency sound waves traveled a shorter distance, but it created a far more detailed sound picture for the dolphin. Or, the dolphin could use a low-frequency click resulting in a lower note that traveled a far greater distance but lacked the sharply defined return sound image.

How do we know all these things? How do we know for example, that when a dolphin echolocates he broadcasts the sound through his melon, rather than say, his larynx? The answers to these and to all such questions were learned only through the work of such people as Kenneth Norris, who ran many painstaking tests on dolphins in captivity. Norris, who pioneered work in dolphin sonar, performed much of his research on a dolphin named Zippy. To demonstrate that this dolphin's sonar definitely did not originate in the larynx as was earlier believed, Norris blindfolded Zippy using soft rubber suction cups over the dolphin's eyes. Then he studied how the animal could locate food without being able to see it visually.

In his experiments, Norris learned that, if food was anywhere above Zippy's beak, she always found it. This indicated that the sounds were emanating from somewhere above, in the upper head. To localize their source even further, researchers found, with the aid of hydrophones, that these high frequency click "trains" (or high speed series of clicks) reached their greatest intensity just ahead of and over her snout.

This indicated that the melon was most probably the source of the emanations. Norris and his assistants fashioned a kind of helmet that would mask that part of the dolphin's head and therefore cancel out the transmissions. But at this point Zippy stopped cooperating. Each time the scientists tried to put on the mask, she shook her head violently and flipped it off. But to show them that there were no hard feelings, she would pick it up in her teeth and obligingly hand it back to the experimenters.

Such were the kinds of setbacks Norris and all such investigators were constantly confronted with in dealing with often-temperamental test animals. But somehow, with much patience, the experiments continued, and gradually the bits of evidence mounted until the scientists were able to come to more positive conclusions about how these animals achieved their marvelous feats.

Describing the dolphin's capability to manipulate a second sound beam, Warshall learned that wild dolphins in the open ocean use multiple sound frequencies to listen acoustically at both close and distant ranges. What was so remarkable was how quickly the mammals could do it.

"The dolphins can switch frequencies in less than one-thousandth of a second," said Warshall. "But whether they use high or low frequencies, they can sputter out clicks with incredible rapidity – up to three hundred per second – and still interpret this fast-fire sound echo."

Water conditions often determine the different kinds of sonar employed by the cetaceans, believes Warshall. For example, the sperm whale, living in clear deep seas, probably resorts to the low-frequency signal necessary for that animal's far-reaching deep-water requirements. In comparison, certain species of muddy-river dolphins, which live in murky water most of their lives, sound off with faint but fast-clicking series apparently more useful to them in their shallower, muddier environment.

Analyzing the characteristics of this underwater sound broadcast by cetaceans, investigator Robert McNally observed that echolocation sound waves operate much in the same way as a beam of light. When the light changes by passing through or reflecting off some object, our eye detects this different

characteristic and from it our brain interprets the image.
However, there are differences, said McNally. "For one thing,
[sound] penetrates much better, bending around corners and
passing through things."

Mediums of different densities reflect different sound
echoes; therefore, said Warshall, "If a human diver jumps into
the water with a dolphin, the dolphin can 'see' inside the
diver into the air passages of his lungs and respiratory system.
This is because sonar sight penetrates materials that are
apparently the same density as the water—like human flesh—
and returns different echoes from objects with different
densities. The greater the difference in density, the more easily
sonar can discriminate.

Once the researchers saw and marveled over the
acoustical feats of these marine mammals they began probing
at the mechanics of this mysterious system. These experiments
were funded by the U.S. Navy, which understandably would
like to know precisely how these animals produce and use this
phenomenal ranging system. Indeed, the navies of the world
would like to know all the secrets of cetacean sonar. One can
well imagine what an incredibly sophisticated sensing system
could thus be acquired if it were possible. So far, however,
man has learned enough to be able to duplicate only a few of
the minor miracles nature has bequeathed to these aquatic
mammals.

One of the biggest mysteries for researchers was how an
animal that lacked vocal cords, and therefore had no voice,
could still manage to send out high- or low-frequency rapid-
fire sound signals. The secret seemed to lie in an area at the
top of the dolphin's head; it appeared to have something to do
with air from the animal's lungs being forced into a lipped air
sac located between the dolphin's melon and his blowhole,
where he breathed.

In an effort to unravel the mystery at the University of
California at Santa Cruz, Kenneth Norris X-rayed dolphins

that were emitting click signals. In the resulting films, he
noticed that a nasal plug, a lip was involved.

The process is complicated to explain but here is what
happens in the sound-making organs of the bottlenose
dolphin: When vocalizing underwater, the blowhole is kept
closed. Air from the lungs is forced into an air sac, distending
it. This air is then released back into the lungs causing the
nasal plug to vibrate against its corresponding lip. As bones of
the jaw and brain case reflect it, this sound is shaped and
focused by the dolphin's oil-filled melon, then beamed out in a
ten-degree arc on each side of a midline through the dolphin.
Echoes of those signals are picked up again through the
mammal's melon and through thin oil in the jawbone where
they are transmitted to the cetacean's inner ear. Dolphins can
broadcast and receive signals simultaneously.

Norris figured that shifting air back and forth between it
and the pharynx through the nasal passages produced the
click sounds, causing the nasal plug to vibrate against nasal
bones. A similar series of vibrating sounds, using the same
mechanical principal of one object rubbing against another,
can be produced as follows: at some restaurants and
drugstores, coffee is served in a cone-shaped paper cup
supported by an outside plastic frame containing the handle.
With a full cup of coffee and your fingers curled through this
handle, place your thumb on the edge of the cardboard cup
rim and move your thumb back and forth, rubbing the rim
just hard enough to make it vibrate. Notice how easy it is to
create a whole series of "click trains" by hardly any movement
of your thumb against this surface. Now, think of the dolphin
"thumbing" the firm lip of flesh just inside its blowhole with
its nasal plug and you can understand how its high-speed
click trains are most likely produced, if indeed it is done this
way.

French bio-acoustician Guy Busnel has a slightly different
theory of how these sounds are produced. Busnel believes that
cetaceans bring them about by pinching air as it escapes

through their nasal passages with two or three organs including the nasal plugs. In effect, he believes they are making the sound frequencies in the same way a child might make air escaping from a balloon literally "sing" by pinching it as it escapes through the neck.

Whichever theory is correct; we will probably never entirely explain how these animals have such incredibly precise control over so wide a range of different clicking characteristics. For example, it may take more than human intelligence to comprehend how dolphins can perform such feats as varying the click rates at will, broadcasting up to one thousand or more sounds per second, changing the frequency of the clicks upward or downward while maintaining what sound experts call "the energy peak." Moreover, while broadcasting broad band clicks, dolphins can simultaneously fire off narrow band signals called "whistles," possibly by producing different sounds at the same time in each nasal passage.

# CHAPTER 5

# Gifted Beyond Belief

During the first year of their birth dolphins develop a whistle name. It not only identifies who they are to other dolphins but it contains enough information to tell who their mother is. You can go on-line and see videos of this. Notice how the whistle sound as though a bird is making them but rather than being sharp and short, they continue with the dolphins.

These mammals have seemingly unlimited memories. Researchers have found that a dolphin can remember the whistle name of another dolphin that they have not seen in more than 20 years. To communicate between themselves and another dolphin they first imitate that dolphin's name and once in contact they 'talk.'

They travel in pods or groups that can number from a few dolphins to many. They don't swim closely together but often they stay further apart in which case their whistle rate increases.

As we all know dolphins often leap from the water surface, sometimes actually somersaulting in the air. This is apparently done for a variety of reasons such as expending energy, or to speed up. If they roll in and out of the water as they swim, this is often called "porpoising, since it imitates the usual swimming action of their cousins, the porpoises. There can be several reasons for them to roll or jump in the air. They may be orienting themselves to things that they can see on the surface; or to speed up. But it may also be done to herd prey; to signal others in the pod, or they may jump just for the joy of it.

We know that dolphins enjoy a playful behavior. In captivity they often pick up objects and bump them around an area. Everything can be a toy to the clever dolphin. Even something as simple as a piece of seaweed. They have been observed bumping a piece around with their noses called beaks, catching it with their fins and just having fun whenever they are in a playful mood. This means pretty much all of the time especially for the youngsters. In captivity a floating rubber ring provides them with endless play opportunities.

Sometimes a toy becomes such a favorite with dolphins that they may keep it with them for days, tucked under a fin so they can play with it whenever they feel like it. Others have been observed blowing bubble rings and playing with them.

This bubble ring is really a vortex of swirling water; a circle of air bubbles swirling in on itself as it moves through the water. The dolphin tosses it around with his beak until it swirls away; then puffs out another one to play with. As a youngster I was fascinated to see my Dad blow smoke rings the same way. Thanks to the Internet we can see this curious activity with the dolphins by using this link on Youtube:

https://www.youtube.com/watch?v=y9JZ4SubOmw

All members of the whale family are apparently able to blow swirling vortices of air. You can also see videos of these. And as a youngster with my first Christmas chemistry set the directions on how to make a "Ray Gun" that 'shot' an invisible 'bullet' of air, fascinated me.

Here's how: First you use the can-opener to cut the bottom out of an empty coffee can. Then you stretch a thin circle of inner tube rubber over the bottom and secured it with wraps of strong string around the edges so it becomes a drum. Into this drum you put an ice cube-sized piece of dry ice. [In my day it could be begged at my local drug store.] Then you point the empty end of your 'ray gun' at a candle burning about 6 feet away. By snapping a finger against the drumhead you will extinguish the candle flame!

Pure Magic? That's what it appears to be. But snapping the drumhead sent an invisible whirling vortex of carbon dioxide gas from the melting dry ice at the flame extinguishing it.

As a budding boy scientist I thought a modern version of my invisible ray gun might be great for shooting down enemy aircraft. [For me WW2 was going on] It still might since no one seems to have followed up on it. Only the clever dolphins learned a practical use for those easily blown homemade whirling bubble-rings no longer invisible underwater. I checked on line to see what might be available for today's budding kid scientists and found detailed instructions on how to make a big 21$^{st}$-Century-vortex-ray-shooting-cannon that was too complicated for me to follow. But coffee cans are still with us. Problem is, the inner tube rubber we get from you-know-where today doesn't have the same bounce to it that our rubber had when we were kids. But innovative weapons are still of interest so if you can figure it out it may be worth a try.

Dolphins have a mischievous side to them. They have been seen coming up under seabirds sitting calmly on the surface, and pulling them under, then letting them go. In the water they play with dogs and humans for no other reason than for the fun of it. They have been known to harass other species, grabbing onto the fluke of a humpback whale just to see if they can get a reaction. Sometimes what they do may be puzzling to us.

For example young dolphins off the coast of Western Australia have been seen chasing as well as capturing and chewing on blowfish. These are also called pufferfish and porcupine fish because some of their kinds are covered with sharp spines. Normally scuba divers see them un-puffed, or deflated. They commonly hang out around shipwrecks and other underwater structures for protection. I've never seen dolphins mess with them but mischievous divers often do. If

you tease a puffer he swells up three or four times his normal
size by inhaling lots of water. Of course fully inflated he is
much larger and looks like a fearsome threatening pincushion
so that molesters will leave him alone.

As soon as the fish feels safe he dumps all that water and
resumes his harmless looking small self again. Orientals value
the puffer for his flavor. In Japan he is considered a delicacy.
A two-tined fork is used to remove the supposedly delicious
meat from his back. The danger of this species lies in its
poisonous liver. It is said that the pufferfish are sometimes
cooked and eaten by Orientals bent on committing Hara-kiri.
What dolphins get out of their interest in Puffers is a mystery.
But some think maybe they chew up these creatures just to get
a high off their poison. Those who know such things tell us
the poison in the fish's skin may intoxicate them temporarily.

Our studies of these mammals have led to the
understanding that dolphins are capable of unusual abilities.
For example they are known to be able to teach, cooperate,
learn, scheme, and grieve. Their brains are larger than human
brains. Researchers have found that in the neo-cortex many
species retain elongated spindle neurons that before 2007 were
known to exist only in humans. These cells have to do with
one's social conduct, emotions, judgment, and were once
thought reserved only for the higher intellectuals such as
humans. Their presence suggests that these animals of high
intellect are capable of the same functions as we are.

The brain size of these mammals is considered an
indicator of their higher intelligence. Since most of the brain is
concerned with our body functions, we believe the same is
true with these mammals. We think animals with large brains
possess a sense of self-awareness. This is a highly developed
sign of thinking in the animal world.

The test researchers use to determine the degree of self-
awareness in these mammals is called the mirror test. A
mirror is shown to the animal and the animal is then marked
with a temporary dye. If that animal goes to the mirror in

order to see that mark, it indicates that he is aware of himself. Those that fail to react this way supposedly mean that they are oblivious to self and are therefore intellectually inferior. Dolphins were quick to see how they looked in the mirror.

Since they are air-breathers, sleeping dolphins in captivity remain close to the surface where a simple reflex of their tail brings them to the surface for a breath of air. Researchers believe that when dolphins sleep only half of their brain is asleep while the other half is on a lookout for trouble. Dolphins in captivity who know they are safe close both eyes and truly appear in deep sleep. Those in the wild where things can happen are thought to grab sleep in snatches while being more wary.

Wild dolphins at sea have few enemies. Among them are the more dangerous to man species of sharks such as the bull sharks, tiger sharks and the great white sharks. These are all potential risks especially for the very young dolphins. Certain species of dolphins that frequent the rivers of the world develop other sleeping patterns. Where currents and debris may be a problem they develop sleeping habits accordingly. For example, where objects such as logs etc. may be moving downstream we believe that the dolphins sleep in short bursts and the rest of the time they are swimming to avoid collisions with the hazards.

Probably the most dangerous threats to dolphins in the wild are our commercial fishermen who use extremely large strong nets to catch such species as schools of large heavyweight tunas.

Once caught in a net where they can't get to the surface to breathe the dolphins drown. Also there are certain nationalities that eat dolphins and butcher them like cattle. Dolphin meat is consumed in a small number of countries worldwide, which include Japan and Peru (where it is referred to as *chancho marino*, or "sea pork"). While Japan may be the best-known and most controversial example, only a very small minority of the population has ever sampled it.

In such places as Queensland, the northeastern quarter of Australia and New South Wales, the southeast quarter of Australia, shark nets and drum lines are used to rid their waters of sharks. These entangle and kill dolphins at the rate of more than a thousand a year. It is estimated that Queensland's shark culling program has killed more than 50,000 sharks since 1962 and in the course this thousands of dolphins are killed along with the sharks and become the so-called bycatch in that country.

Interestingly, in Greek Mythology dolphins were commonly seen as helpers to mankind. It is equally true with Minoans who honored dolphins by including them in their wall paintings showing the dolphins and humans together. These mammals are also popular in Greek Mythology and many poems in Greece feature men or boys or deities riding on the backs of dolphins. And the ancient Greeks welcomed these mammals because they saw them riding in the wakes of their ships where they were always considered, a good omen.

The dolphin is also present in their art. Cupid is often shown riding a dolphin and it became a belief down through the centuries that dolphins always came to the rescue of humans lost at sea. Stories abound in which they supposedly fought off sharks and helped push survivors toward ashore. These friendly mammals have always been such a good luck symbol that the figure of a dolphin often appeared in coats of arms. Legendary tales of their noble character in being helpful to man occurs throughout our history.

For dolphins in captivity as performer their antics have always entertained generations of people from around the world. The same is true of killer whales that are in the same family. But more efforts are being made to liberate these noble creatures rather than to keep them captive for our amusement.

Organizations such as Florida's Mote Marine Laboratory rescue and rehabilitate sick, wounded, stranded or orphaned dolphins while other groups such as The Whale and Dolphin Conservation and Hong Kong Dolphin Conservation Society conserve and protect the Ganges River dolphin and other species that live under stressful conditions.

Our military has used trained dolphins to perform special underwater jobs such as helping to locate lost underwater military equipment. During the Vietnam War it was rumored that the U.S, Navy trained dolphins to kill enemy divers. The U.S. Navy denied that at any time were dolphins trained for combat. But they are still being trained for other tasks as part of the U.S. Navy Marine Mammal Program.

Dolphins are increasingly our popular choice of animal-assisted therapy for psychological problems and other disabilities. A study found that dolphins were an effective treatment for mild to moderate depression, but the calming affect lasted only as long as the encounter.

**CHAPTER 6**

# Secrets Behind the Dolphin Smile

Based on fossil evidence, scientists believe that dolphins and whales, the family of air-breathing mammals we call cetaceans, were once land animals that walked on four legs. Related to today's hippos, 50 million years ago they evolved into sea creatures. To understand how these air-breathing mammals of our water world comprehend their environment you would have to forget what you see but sharpen what you hear. Sight is our primary sense. Hearing is theirs. To be like them what you hear your brain would process into sound pictures and store them in your brain for future reference.

You would recognize other creatures in your world by the sounds they made or by the echoes you get back from the sounds *you made*. Everything about where you are and who you are and who is with you would all be based on sound. That would be your primary sense. In the dark or if you closed your eyes you would instantly know everything around you as if you saw it with your eyes. But air-breathing animals like whales and dolphins need not see visually because they "see" it all with their sense of sound.

As noted, these remarkable marine air-breathers can perform feats that we human animals of "higher" intelligence can only marvel at. Here is another example:

A dolphin is asked to tell the difference between two pieces of metal painted the same color, one a square of copper and the other a square of brass. Always the dolphin easily picks the copper square from the brass square even though both targets look exactly alike.

Even more amazing, a blindfolded dolphin can instantly "see" you in the water with him; he can also tell things about your internal makeup that only a doctor might otherwise determine with an X-ray.

How is it possible for these marine animals to perform such astounding feats? This is one of the questions researcher Kenneth Norris asked himself upon observing how well dolphins in captivity were able to solve such seemingly unsolvable problems.

It was as if the animals were capable of reading the experimenter's mind, as if they possessed some kind of super sense that replaced their sight so that even though blindfolded they could "see" the tiny targets researchers were asking them to identify.

Thanks to the continued efforts of such early researchers as Norris, we now know that dolphins do indeed possess a super sense, a sound sense that among other things allows them to pinpoint targets through what we now call echolocation. It is the system whales and dolphins use as their sonar (Sound Navigation and Ranging) systems, even when blindfolded.

Researchers learned that the fatty tissue in the dolphin's forehead, the melon, was capable of focusing this sound – literally beaming it out in different directions, the same way you might beam a spotlight into the darkness to illuminate some object. But astonishingly enough, with the dolphin these echolocation patterns were not only broadcast out at a normal ten degree arc from either side of a midline down the animal's head, but the animal also could shape the beam, make it broader or narrower, or even project a second beam at an angle to the first.

For wide coverage the mammal had only to swing its head from side to side. Moreover, the beam could be fine-tuned. A high-pitched note made up of shortly spaced high-frequency sound waves traveled a shorter distance, but it created a far more detailed sound picture for the dolphin. Or, the dolphin could use a low-frequency click resulting in a lower note that traveled a far greater distance but lacked the sharply defined return sound image.

Complex and wonderful as the dolphin's sonar system is, man is slowly but surely closing the gap in understanding how it all works and how we may duplicate some of their feats on a smaller scale. As a result of extensive inquiries into the mechanics of cetacean sonar, scientists today are using side-scan sonar systems to actually draw three-dimensional pictures of such things as underwater shipwrecks in the deepest part of the ocean. Or, they can actually look through the bottom of the ocean, penetrating the less dense material to bounce signals back from denser objects that may lie hidden beneath the substrate.

More recently, thanks to scientists using these seemingly magical processes for his own purposes we now have LiDAR (Light Detection and Ranging) a remote sensing technology that uses the pulse from a laser to collect measurements which can then be used to create 3D models and maps of objects and environments.

LiDAR technology has been around since the 1960's when laser scanners were mounted to airplanes. But it wasn't until the late 1980's, with the introduction of commercially viable GPS systems, that LiDAR data became a useful tool for providing accurate information identifying natural and unnatural or manmade features on earth. For instance when LiDAR looked at the dense jungles of Central America from the air it revealed thousands of manmade Mayan stone structures we never knew were there.

"Our present electronic equipment can't match a dolphin's abilities – not by a factor of ten," said Richard Soule, director of the Biosystems Division of the U.S. Naval Oceans Systems Center Laboratory in Hawaii. The dolphins are still ahead of us, but in this computer age, we are fast catching up.

While naval research scientists try to imitate the dolphins super-sonar system, other investigators seek to comprehend another puzzling sound made by the mammals – a pure tone emission that researchers call "whistles," which scribe sonograms showing trills, vibratos, and glissandos, sound pictures that look astonishingly like sonograms made of bird calls. Researchers believe these are sound signals employed by the dolphins to communicate certain kinds of information to each other. Scientific eavesdroppers counted some two thousand different whistles emanating from dolphins in captivity.

"On that basis," said Jacques Cousteau, "one might conclude that the language of the dolphins is composed of two thousand sounds – or we might say, two thousand 'words.' "

But those who listened and recorded soon learned that these sounds were not always the same, nor to the observers did they seem to have any meaning to the mammals. Only later did researchers learn that these sounds were the dolphin's name that identified him or her to all the others.

Efforts to study communication between dolphins are further complicated by their lack of the kind of external expressions commonly found in such land animals as chimpanzees or even dogs. A wagging canine tail, for example, speaks volumes. Even facial expressions are a form of "paralanguage" – the lips drawn back in a snarl, teeth bared, the low rumbling growl – and they leave no question in our minds as to the message the animal wishes to convey: "Watch out. I may attack you!"

But with the comparatively stiff-bodied, fixed expression so common to the dolphins, scientists involved in communication studies are limited when they look to the dolphin for any real 'body language' and yet, these animals do possess a body language, subtle, as it may seem.

The angle at which a dolphin may hold its body is meaningful to another dolphin. It may say such things as, "Watch out. I've had enough of your foolishness." When one dolphin confronts another from the front, opening its mouth and arching its back, this, say observers, is a threatening gesture. Conversely, when a dolphin closes its mouth and turns its body sideways, this is interpreted as a sign of submission.

It is also believed that dolphins are capable of resolving differences in the pattern of their pigmentation, enabling them to identify species at a distance and individuals at close range.

Touching is another form of communication among the cetaceans; these aquatic mammals use it in much the same way it is by land animals. This is particularly true in the relationship and tactile bond between infant and parent, as well as in the mating ritual.

It is unfortunate that almost all emphasis of our cetacean research has been directed largely toward trying to crack the mystery of their echolocation (sonar) system, the area of greatest interest to the Navy and therefore the area of greatest funding for research. Only in very limited and isolated cases has some experimental work been done in the area of communication, with studies designed to reveal the intelligence of these animals. Despite the many popular written and filmed treatments of this subject, we still have few hardcore facts to go on. But as we gradually begin to understand more about the extent of communication between these marine animals, the next question some scientists asked was, "Can we communicate with them?"

# CHAPTER 7

# Communicating with Dolphins

"To actually live with a dolphin twenty-four hours a day is a very taxing situation. Much more so than I had anticipated. Unlike a dog, unlike a cat, unlike a human, a dolphin is more like a shadow than a roommate. If given the opportunity, he will never leave your physical being."

Thus wrote Margaret C. Howe in a special report detailing the events of living with Peter, a full-grown male *Tursiops truncatus* dolphin, in a special pool built for the two of them at the Dolphin Point Laboratory of the Communications Research Institute at St. Thomas, U.S. Virgin Islands, in 1965. This was one of the most unique experiments ever conducted to see if it were possible for humans to communicate with dolphins on a higher level than ever before achieved. This line of research originated with Dr. John C. Lilly, whose efforts from the mid-1950s on led to the development of the Dolphin Communication Laboratory at St. Thomas.

The initial proposal was for Miss Howe to live in close contact with Peter for a period of two and a half months. During this time, the human researcher was to attempt to establish a communication level with the dolphin that would include a personal relationship and she hoped, vocal exchanges.

By this time it was known that dolphins could mimic sounds they heard not only in their environment, but in ours as well. What impressed researchers, however, was that these mimicked sounds could be made out of water through the dolphin's blowhole and in frequencies which we humans could hear. It was believed by some that the reason the mammals produced these "humanoids," as Dr. Lilly came to call them, was solely for humans to hear. Certainly, they said, such sounds were not produced for their own kind. Thus began the research to determine just how adept a dolphin might be at developing this ability to mimic human speech. The Virgin Island laboratory seemed ideal for the experiment. Portions of the facility were modified in such a way and with great forethought to make both participants in this experiment as comfortable as possible. In the flooded "house" part, Miss Howe would sleep on a bed elevated inches above the water level where she could still maintain contact with the dolphin swimming in the two-foot-deep water of the main living area. This room opened by way of a half-Dutch-door arrangement into a flooded veranda containing adequate water for the dolphin to swim in. Strategically located microphones in the house unit would pick up all the vocal exchanges of the participants and would be tape-recorded. Miss Howe could also do her own cooking by a special kitchen arrangement in the area and could keep a written record of the events on a deck projecting out over the pool.

Before undertaking the two and a half-month experiment, Miss Howe spent seven days and seven nights living with Pam, a female dolphin, to see exactly what problems might need remedying before undertaking the long-term project. This particular dolphin had had several traumatic experiences that made her reluctant to engage in any close relationships with humans. According to Dr. Lilly, during the filming of the movie *Flipper*, a diver had speared the dolphin three times. For over two years now she showed all the symptoms of being a loner, apprehensive of humans and totally unresponsive to efforts made to encourage any kind of close relationship.

During the week of involvement with Miss Howe, however, the traumatized Pam gradually lost some of her fear of humans and developed a freer relationship. Thanks to Miss Howe's urging and skill, Pam reached the point where she could be fed by hand and was beginning to vocalize with the researcher, albeit in "Delphanese," dolphin chatter consisting of clicks, chirps, whistles, and other typically dolphin phonations, rather than the humanoids that mimicked our speech.

Later, during the actual two-and-a-half-month-long experiment with Peter, there were times when Miss Howe wished fervently that she had engaged the more docile Pam in this long-term effort, rather than the rambunctious male dolphin that seemed mainly interested in continual play when he should settle down and learn his lessons with his young teacher.

That she was able to carry out this experiment in extreme isolation and at considerable mental and physical discomfort, during which the close relationship necessitated her being wet most of the time, is a credit to Miss Howe's dedication to the project.

At the beginning of the experiment, detailed in its entirety in Dr. Lilly's book *The Mind of the Dolphin* (Doubleday & Co., 1967), the dolphin Peter used only the Delphanese clicking at Miss Howe's request to learn such specific words as ball, Bo-Bo clown, or toy, while playing with the dolphin with these different items. Gradually, however, the dolphin began using a few humanoids, sounds that vaguely resembled words spoken to him by Miss Howe. For example, to the phrase "Hello, Peter," he might include in his clicking the humanoid "Oh" sound. Also, toward the end of the experiment it appeared that Peter could alternate his responses with the researcher's requests. When Miss Howe spoke, Peter seemed to listen, then would respond.

In conclusion, however, it appeared that to try to teach dolphins to mimic our speech was not the way to bring about a breakthrough. No one realized this more than Dr. Lilly himself, a man whom many consider the foremost authority on dolphins and proponent of the popular belief that dolphins are of equal or greater intelligence than man and that once we learn how, we will be able to communicate on the most abstract levels with them.

How did we come to this belief in the first place? The idea is not particularly new. It gained considerable momentum in the mid-1950s, when we learned that such animals as dolphins were capable of emitting sounds in the air that sometimes sounded strangely like the sounds they had heard in our world. We realized then that they were able to mimic sounds, imitating not only such things as a generator humming near their tank, but also human words that were spoken to them. Moreover, scientists such as Dr. John Lilly, while studying the anatomy of these marine mammals, were quick to notice that the dolphins brain was astonishingly similar to the human brain and weighed only a bit more – 1600 grams to our 1400-gram organ. No other animal on earth has a brain so similar to ours while maintaining a comparatively similar body weight. Was it possible, then, that this marine mammal with incredible sonar capabilities might be taught to share a give and take of thoughts and ideas with us? That was the first question that came to Dr. Lilly's mind.

Outside the academic community other equally diligent, if not quite so scientific, researchers experimented with human/dolphin relationships based almost entirely on an intimate, personal, emotional encounter with the animals. One such individual was Malcolm Brenner of Sarasota, Florida. Brenner's curiosity to learn about dolphins brought him to them. He began a close personal relationship with a female dolphin named Ruby. As far as Brenner was concerned, he achieved contact, and achieved an interspecies romance with this affectionate animal.

In an early episode involving his relationship with this dolphin, Brenner detailed an experience not uncommon among other dolphin observers who have had extremely close relationships with these animals as trainers, owners, or individuals seeking to go beyond the normal bounds of a trainer/dolphin encounter. Dr. Lilly first recognized the phenomenon in his work with dolphins in 1955, 1957, and 1958. In 1962 he described it as "a feeling of weirdness." As he said, it was the feeling that one was in the presence of something or someone of considerable intelligence waiting just on the other side of a nebulous barrier one was trying to penetrate. On that other side was an intelligent being that was trying just as hard as you were to breach the barrier, to communicate, and to reach you."

This is the essence of Brenner's observations, made quite accidentally and unscientifically. It occurred one cold March day when the dolphin enticed Brenner into her pool for an informal romp together. The water was ice cold to Brenner, who was in no mood to stay there very long. But Ruby seemed to be saying, "Come on in, the water's fine. We'll have a good time."

So in he went. There followed a tooth-chattering interlude for Brenner as the dolphin swam increasingly faster circles around him, almost frightening him with her violent activity. Ruby was apparently excited by his presence. She nuzzled him repeatedly, checked him up and down with her sonar, and whenever he reached out to stroke her, she allowed only so much familiarity, then retreated, just out of hand's reach, enticing him further into the pool. There, she nuzzled him, indicating that she was in the mood for play. But it was cold. Brenner stayed in the water as long as he could, then he had to get out.

Spotting her ball near the pool, Brenner decided it was a good opportunity to use Ruby's fondness for a game of catch as a reward to see if he could persuade her to mimic her name. He threw the ball to her and she quickly threw it back. They did this several times. The dolphin was enjoying the interchange enormously. Then, Brenner withheld the ball and said, "Come on Ruby, say Rooo-beee, like that. Come on. You can do it. Say Rooo-beee."

Instead, Ruby squeaked Delphanese in reply to Brenner.

"No, no," Brenner said. "That's not it. Say Rooo-beee." He

held up the ball, withholding the reward.

As he continued urging her to pronounce her name, he suddenly became aware that her squawks had changed considerably. The sound was now distinctly two syllables. Nothing significant except that the two syllables were sounding strangely like those he had just been repeating for her. In response and as a reward for this, Brenner threw the cherished ball to the dolphin. In minutes he realized that she was beginning to copy the same speech pattern that he was using, even to the inflections of his voice, to mimic the very word he had been saying – " Rooo-beee."

Brenner was amazed that she had picked it up so quickly. Each time her pronunciation seemed less like his, he withheld the ball. Whenever Ruby replied with a sound that more closely imitated her name, he responded with the ball reward. He said, "We stood a few feet apart in the water of her pen, staring at each other intently with bright eyes and the excitement between us was palpable. Never in my life had I known such an intimate feeling of being in contact with an incredibly nonhuman creature. It felt like it was what I had been created to do. Our minds seemed to be running on the same wave. We were together!"

What astonished Brenner most was that all of this had happened in less than ten minutes! After a while, however, it appeared that perhaps Ruby had become bored with the game. She pronounced her name as clearly as Brenner thought she could a couple of times, then stopped and babbled at him in Delphanese, accompanying this with a vigorous nodding up and down of her head, a gesture Brenner knew was associated with pleasure and which he called "ya-ya-ing." Then, she suddenly swam back a few feet, rose up out of water and emitted a peculiar noise that sounded to Brenner like "Keee-orr-oop" three times in short staccato deliveries.

Brenner said he did not know why, but it occurred to him to repeat the sound to Ruby, which he did as best he could. This effort was not as good as Ruby's, but she seemed to be expecting it of him. So Brenner tried. Ruby repeated the sound, but this time it too sounded different. She had modified it slightly. Brenner did likewise, responding by repeating the word with its modifications to Ruby, again, as best he could with the inadequacy of human lips and vocal cords. She repeated the sound and again it was still a little different. Once more Brenner mimicked this difference, saying, "Kee-orr-oop."

"Suddenly," he reported later, "the light in my head went on. The sound I had just successfully imitated was the one she had been giving me in the beginning in response to my first attempts to make her say, 'Ruby! "

Brenner realized this the instant the word was coming out of his lips and he said a whole bunch of fuses seemed to go off inside his head with the realization. He did a double take, staring at Ruby who seemed, he said, to be watching him with great concentration. "When she saw the double-take and knew I knew, she flipped out and went yo-yoing around the pool, throwing water into the air very excited and apparently happy that this two-legged cousin of hers was progressing so rapidly."

What was the meaning of this experience, Brenner asked himself. Quickly, he reviewed what had happened. He had given the dolphin an English word – her name, Ruby – to pronounce. In response to it Ruby had replied with a Delphanese word or phrase that Brenner had at first ignored. But then through the ensuing interchange, during which he allowed himself to become the pupil rather than the teacher, there was some kind of progress. Brenner felt that each knew that the other knew what had transpired and it was this awareness, this "weird feeling," of Dr. Lilly's that had so impressed Brenner.

Certainly he knew that Ruby was smart enough to recognize her human name. But what was the significance of the sounds she repeated in return, he wondered. Could this possibly have been Ruby's Delphanese name for him? Or was it just the opposite; was she repeating her own Delphanese name? Brenner was fully aware that these were nothing more than his own projections of what he had heard. Still, it bothered him.

Months later, when he tried to coax Ruby to mimic her name for other observers, he was less successful. But she did manage to enunciate "Rooo-beee" once or twice. She seemed restless, impatient, as if being asked to do this mundane trick simply bored her. Brenner thought he understood why. He knew that dolphin trainers were aware of the dolphin's low threshold for boredom, that once they learned a trick they would repeat it only so often – then they were ready to go on to something new.

Years later, when Brenner told a scientist about this experience with Ruby, his contention was that it was "too bad he had not tape-recorded the interchange, that so often one hears what he wants to hear from an animal from which he is trying to elicit a favorable response. Besides," said the scientist, "one hears of this sort of thing so often."

If this were the case, Brenner wondered why scientists did not try squawking Delphanese to dolphins more often. Maybe, in fact, humans were the real ones slowing down the communication between man and dolphin. Maybe it was not so much a case of their not being able to understand our language as it was our inability, and as yet, unwillingness, to try to understand theirs. Meanwhile, if any further research is done we may have to go into their world to do it.

# CHAPTER 8

# WHEN DOLPHINS CAME:
## The Story of 'Boy'

*(In September 1965, as hurricane Betsy sliced a swath across the Gulf of Mexico to sideswipe Florida, Mississippi, and Louisiana, two bottlenose dolphins seeking refuge from the storm swam through northwest Florida's narrow Philip's Inlet into large and partially brackish Powell Lake. This story is based on that event.)*

*This story is warmly dedicated
To the Memory of 'Boy' the dolphin
To George and Etta our friends
To Julia Ann my lovely wife
To Smokey Joe our kittycat
To Tisha our faithful dog and
To Chita our little lively monkey
All who were with me for
This adventure that took place
Once upon a time*

# Storm Flight

At first only blue filled the void, stretching endlessly in all directions, shifting shades from deep indigo up through the spectrum to the silvery surface blue. Between these two extremes appeared two rapidly moving sleek gray shapes. In perfect unison they traveled a loping course as if riding astride some swift jet stream in that unlimited blue galaxy. Flowing through the ocean with unerring accuracy of direction, two bottlenose dolphins, a male and a female, kept close contact with each other as they sonar-scanned the distant voids ahead.

Both maintained the same position they had held since they felt the swift change in barometric pressure, the male above and slightly ahead of the female so she had the advantage of his slipstream. She had merely to lift her head to touch him reassuringly with the smooth oil-filled melon of her dome. It was a touch she used frequently at such times as this, when they were under stress.

He in turn regulated his speed so as not to swim so swiftly she would grow fatigued. Yet he knew the danger of not achieving their goal in time. Both had read the signs of the oncoming storm that was trying to cut off their retreat to safer waters. Unlike the great whales and sharks, these air-breathing mammals could not dive into the safety of the deep. They had to stay in shallow waters where they could breathe.

This was no ordinary storm, one they might enjoy playing in, hurling themselves from the crashing waves in wild flights of ecstasy. This storm soon consumed the sky and the ocean behind them in its black fury. Its winds would grow so powerful few living things could long endure its wrath. Only the deep provided protection from such storms as this. Now it threatened to catch them close to shore where the water over the shelf would soon become a death trap.

But that was the only refuge that might still remain open to them. Both knew it well from a lifetime of venturing along this coast. It was an inlet, a narrow, shallow pass through the shoals, the only one for hundreds of miles along this coast. If they could reach it and swim through into the deep brackish bay before the storm made it impossible to cross the shoals, they would be safe.

But could they make it in time? The dolphins knew that such storms moved fast as the wind, faster than they could swim.

For a while it had been behind them, then it was surrounding them. Now, like an evil thing it was trying to block their final escape. The female found it better not to look anymore; not to worry about its consequences. Whatever happened, she would stay with her mate.

At their last surface sighting he saw the seething black malevolence in the heavens on each side of them, reaching out with its swirling black shapes to engulf them like the lobes of a giant manta. But unlike that friendly giant, this sky manta was to be feared. Even now the male saw the lobes closing ahead of them joining in a rapidly thickening coiled wall between them and the distant shore.

They were in its eye. Directly beneath the blackest of the storm barrier, seas over the rocky shallows would be totally wild. At its worse, the churning water and sand would become one, a thick slurry where no living thing could survive, where only the sharp shoals remained unmoved, hidden by the fury, waiting to met out death and destruction to whatever chanced their way.

Still the dolphins knew they had no choice but to hurry on, to try and make the pass before the worst of the storm overwhelmed them. The male wanted it more than ever for her and for his unborn pup she bore. He increased his speed, driving with more determination now that they approached the dangerous area. As he speeded up, so did his mate, instantly aware of his growing urgency.

Continually both dolphins sounded the severely changing conditions ahead of them, beaming their ultrasonic probes at the rate of 300 clicks per second while the incredible computer capabilities of their large brains simultaneously evaluated the returning echoes slightly altered now by the turbulence ahead. Normally their periodic flash through the surface to gasp a breath made them but a blur in the growing fury of slathering seas. But now even the female knew what she had sensed but refused to accept earlier. The storm had beat them. Its churning black clouds, high winds and torrential rains were already pounding the coasts ahead.

Below the sea's surface they entered a growing maelstrom. No longer could they see clear blue distance. The water thickened with swirling sand driven by powerful currents. For protection, they closed their eyes, having no need to see their surroundings as they raced through the darkening void. But in their mind's eye they saw it all, the rapidly shoaling bottom; the patches of sharp exposed lime-rock ridges. Each outcropping was but another familiar signpost to them, the same kind of signposts they had been following from far at sea. Heaven and earth told them all they needed to know. In the open ocean the stars had been their guides. Underwater their sonar picked out similar familiar guides. Tracing the configurations of the bottom they read the ancient way-signs – the particular sea mounts, the old coral ridges, the rise and fall of the contoured bottom – all imparted specific information as to their whereabouts.

Now, even in the altered nature of their surroundings they picked up another vital clue, one that spurred them into even greater bursts of speed. It was the taste of the sea. On the taste buds at the base of their tongues they caught the faint taste of freshwater mingling with the more apparent flavor of tannin. They were on course, homing in on the distant bay, approaching the brackish, tannin-tainted outflow precisely on target.

But now, suddenly, conditions worsened. Though they continued sounding ahead to avoid possible collisions, the shoaling seas became almost too much for them. Giant waves crashed against each other in such chaotic confusion that they were soon being heaved this way and that by the powerful forces. When they split the surface to snatch a breath of air, it was as if even the air had become part of the sea. Still they raced on, vainly trying to swim through the colliding currents while maintaining as much of their equilibrium as possible.

It was unbelievably difficult. The seas were pure sand slurries now. It was shallow now. The jagged limestone outcroppings were just below them now. Repeatedly the seas surge slammed them to the bottom and ruthlessly tumbled them over the sharp, unyielding rocks. But side-by-side they hurled themselves on toward the elusive opening despite the harsh slashing cuts and abrasions suffered whenever the combined forces caught them in their fury. After one particularly dreadful mauling, the female began to lag behind, unable to keep up.

"Only a short way now," signaled the female to her mate. But even though her sonic message was meant to reassure him, the male noted that her pulsed signals were not normal.

Immediately he dropped back to help. Close by her flank he saw with growing alarm that she had been severely cut and lacerated all over her extremities. Worst of all was a long jagged gash extending from just behind her pectoral to far back on her belly, a gash that flowed blood freely.

"Hold on…", he signaled her…. "Only a bit further…." The last was the worst of all. As great holes opened in the seas above them they were hurled across the sharp rock ledges marking the entrance to the channel. Ledges there had been honed to keen edges by years of seesawing currents containing quartz sand until now their hardest parts were razor sharp.

Over the crashing thunder of the surf he heard her sounds mingling with his – the painful gasps, the grinding of flesh against reef, the cries of anger he made; the sounds of deep hurt she made.

Then suddenly, the worst was past. They broke through the rocky barrier into a deep meandering channel whose sides of sand rose high on either side of them. The sweet water taste was very strong now, the bay's depths no longer seething storms of sand, but calmer.

At first, overwhelmed with relief that they had made it, the male sped through the warm, brackish water that soothed rather than stung his lacerated body. Only when he swerved back for her did he abruptly lose his exuberance. He saw her trailing behind because she was hurt more than he had thought. Her entire body was lacerated and she was laboring.

Immediately he was beside her. Their bodies touched. He helped her as best he could; doing what he could to buoy her up and help her swim. There was no need to hurry now. They were entering the deep bay. She, however, was strangely silent. She had not responded to his sounds of concern over her condition. But then it was unnecessary. He saw what the sharp ledges had done to her body. He saw her swimming movements weakening until they were almost too much effort for her to surface without him nudging her upward to gasp air.

Above them the storm raged but the worst had passed overhead. It was moving inland fast. Now rather than the water being a sand slurry, the air filled with sand. The protective dunes lost their crests. Like ocean waves their tops melted away as though being consumed my some invisible sand-eating monster.

Before leaving the sheltering dunes the channel broadened to include several large sand deltas devoid of growth. They were formed early that spring when the pass had sanded in and the backwaters of the bay built up. Finally the accumulation of dark brown tannin-stained water forced the channel open again and in this annual flushing of the waterway, these sand islands remained.

Here, the male dolphin brought her to rest. The water was shallow and warm. The female no longer needed to struggle to the surface to breathe. She lay beside him, their backs out of water, their stomachs pressed against the fine brown silt of the bar. The choppy waves splashed over them. Here they would wait, he decided, until she became stronger and they could go on.

The storm could no longer hurt them. Its torrents of wind driven rain only soothed them. Though there was some danger of their being stranded, they were close to deep water and the tides would be so swollen by the storm that they would be no problem.

Through the night the storm savaged the land and sea. The worst of it passed in the howling gales of darkness that prevailed until noon the next day. The two dolphins had remained beside the sand bars throughout the first day and night. They had eaten nothing now for almost two days. Though the female had no pain, the male dolphin saw she was weaker.

He would hunt and find them food. Schools of frightened mullet would be nearby. Food was what she needed. He would bring her back mullet and it would make her feel better. When the male dolphin told her this, the female hardly responded. She had no desire to eat but insisted he go find food to keep up his own strength.

For a moment he remained beside her, touching her flanks by gently rocking his body back and forth against her. She acknowledged him with deeply murmured sighs of understanding. "Go," she told him. "I will be all right."

Reluctantly, he slid himself into deeper water, then lay with his head toward her but turned so he could see her flanks. Her wounds were still open and pumping faint puffs of blood into the surrounding water. The gaping lacerations were more severe than he had suspected. He scanned her deeper, seeing that all her vital signs were weak but still functioning. I must get her food, he thought, and pushed himself into deep water.

Swimming swiftly he headed for a bend in the bay long remembered as a popular place to hunt mullet. Piled granite rocks were shaped by man into a long jetty paralleling the shore. The front faced the deepwater channel. Behind it the sand shoaled to provide a protective lagoon where the flashing silver schools of mullet often came to feed and to hide from the net boats that were unable to work this narrow lagoon. The fish would be there now, coming from the depths of the bay where they had ridden out the storm. They would be as hungry as he.

As the dolphin swam around the jumbled rocks at the jetty entrance, his sonar scan provided him with a perfect picture of his quarry. They were there as he suspected. Most of them packed into the back and more panicky than he had thought. The school was split in two, both groups moving nervously back and forth. A swift side-scan picked up a string of stragglers on his right flank. Their movements were less hurried. They were feeding on the green moss growing on the rocks. They had not seen nor sensed him yet. The dolphin was not interested in those. The schools packed in the background were more to his liking. Directly behind them the steeply sloped sand and mud banks were just right for what he planned.

Now he moved like a swift shadow, sweeping in on the schools from one side, releasing a solid stream of bubbles from his breathing vent while vibrating the fleshy lip to create a loud raucous underwater sound.

The mullet flashed into a compact group that darted into the shallows to avoid whatever horrendous thing had suddenly slashed across their line of view like a load of thrown cast net leads trailing bubbles behind its deadly nylon mesh. And at that instant of mistaken reflex, he was upon them, a rushing giant in their midst that sent them flying out of water onto the bank. And he was there too, snatching them from right and left as they struggled vainly on the steep wet banks.

Slowly he slipped back into the lagoon, sighted the second school and once again brought them back together with a resounding smack of his flukes on the surface. Then again the rush, the drive up the bank and the gulping of mullet as he slowly slid into the water. This time he did not eat his fill but carried three of them in his snout as he left the lagoon to the now thoroughly scattered and panicky fish.

As the dolphin swept back toward the sandbar, he mouthed the mullet, breaking their backs, softening them so they would be less difficult for the female to consume. She was lying in the same position where he had left her. But as he approached, he realized something was different. From a distance he scanned her and it was then he knew, though he still refused to believe it.

Swiftly he swam to her side, nudging her. He placed the mullet beside her closed jaws. He repeatedly tried to get her to respond but she could not. No matter what he did, she showed no signs of life. Still, the male dolphin refused to believe what all his senses were telling him. She had been alive moments ago. Her vital signs were not that bad. How could she have weakened so quickly? Surely it was something else. All he had to do was get her to breathe again and she would be all right.

He got on the other side of her and began pushing with his head. Slowly she began to move. He threw all of his weight behind the effort, heaving himself against her, pushing and shoving, gaining ground gradually as she slid closer to the deeper water at the end of the bar.

Finally he had her afloat. He took her flipper gingerly in his snout as they had done so many times before in their play. But now he tugged her without feeling the slightest resistance, not a tremor of response.

Undaunted, the male dolphin swam with her along the surface of the bay, chattering to her, encouraging her, gently nudging her belly to get her to breathe. But nothing he did brought any response from her lifeless form. He remained with her in this manner for the next three hours, the two of them moving in a strange slow motion duet across the choppy waters of the bay. Then, he returned with her to the sand bar. He nudged her body into a position where the rising tide would soon claim it.

That evening, when the tide changed and the brackish water flowed heavily out through the inlet, she would go with it back to the sea.

When the male dolphin turned away from the sandbar this time, it was not to make his way out through the pass the way they had come. When he remembered how it had been, how many things they had shared together, he now had no desire to return without her…without them. They were both gone to him now. There was not much reason to go anywhere anymore.

The grieving male swam slowly back along the channel and into the bay. He swam beneath a long concrete bridge and continued swimming aimlessly up the widening body of browning water. On the distant shores rose tier upon tier of pine trees interspersed with occasional houses. But these things made no more impression on him than the fact that the heavy gray skies were gradually clearing and the storm was finally coming to an end.

All winter long the dolphin remained in the bay. The northwest Florida winter was so cold that fish he fed on sometimes swam far up the shallow water tributaries of the bay and expired there. This fact was of little importance to the dolphin. To him they were nothing but food, something that he now never seemed to have much appetite for.

As the months passed, he lost weight. His days were spent wandering through the empty corridors of this deep, brown featureless world where he had chosen to remain totally alone.

Once in a while his wanderings brought him back to the inlet and the sandbar where he had left her body. As he knew in his heart there would not be, he found no evidence of her ever having been there. Still he nosed around the bar, testing the sand here and there to make absolutely sure. Then, he would turn and swim back once more into the deep empty recesses of the bay.

By midwinter the narrow inlet closed. Sand pushed up along the coast by the steep winter waves did the job it had been doing for countless years. Then came the torrential rains of the early year. Gradually the bay fattened, growing corpulent with the runoff water until the brackish water turned dark brown and reeked of tannin from the leaching of all the organic matter that found its way there. The flavors of tree roots, pine bark, dead leaves and weeds mingled with the chemical excrements of farmers' fields farther inland combined to produce water that was hardly fit for man or beast. And still, even if the pass had been open, the dolphin had no wish to return to the sea.

When at last the warmer days of spring came more frequently to the Gulf coast, a subtle, almost imperceptible change came over the dolphin. Even he, at first, was unaware of it. In place of the hollow emptiness he now began to feel the need for companionship. He wanted a friend.

# Sput, Sput, Sputter

In early May the entire character of the bay changed. The constant warm tropical rains turned the surrounding countryside a vibrant green. Not the green of summer by any means but the fresh new chartreuse green of early spring.

While the pine woods brightened and the wildflowers bloomed color into the grassy glens below the sand dunes, the bay itself tolerated its swollen brown-stained waters until the very last moment. Then, as it always did each spring about the same time, it overflowed its dry sand-clogged inlet.

As the first brown trickle inched its way across the wind-rippled compacted crystals of fine white quartzite sand, the firm barrier was soon breached. Even as it went, the trickle widened and ate itself deeper until it quickly progressed from a narrow stream to a wide waterway and with the full force of the bay behind it now, nothing stopped it from turning into a raging torrent of rushing water.

It was not until long after it had spent its fury against the land in its overpowering eagerness to reach the sea that the flow gradually eased its intensity. There now was a deep channel flowing in one long continuous bisecting line linking the bay with the sea. For a mile the clear blue green Gulf waters along the coast would be stained with that long pent-up affluent. The splotched ugly mushrooming cloud of tannin water always was reluctant to give up its rich mahogany hues for that of the sea. But in the days to come the sea would finally win the battle, reversing the outflow and in repeated tidal exchanges, the bay's waters would finally lose much of their deep color and be cleansed. At least until the next heavy rains came to return the stain again.

With the blooming of the flowers and the brightening of the bay waters, the male dolphin began cruising closer to shore as if searching for something. Day after day he swam along the side of the cove where man had built his long wood docks and habitations. From his vantage point the dolphin saw growing activity on shore. Though he could not understand why, the dolphin found himself drawn to it. His constant curiosity brought him in so close that he often rolled and cavorted under the long docks where he could keep an eye on whatever strange and curious things occurred nearby.

It was on one such surveillance of men sliding a big boat down the bank toward the water that the dolphin was abruptly noticed. A creature suddenly appeared at the end of a dock above him and yapped fiercely at him.

Startled, the dolphin dived with a splash. Surfacing a safer distance away, he eyed the loud-mouthed intruder curiously. Formerly, he had only seen such creatures from afar, loping ahead of man on beaches. Now he studied the strangely spotted animal more closely.

What an unbecoming sound it makes, he thought. Surely meaningless as a language but maybe some kind of salutation. He would return it and see what happened.

Hoisting himself well out of water the dolphin squeezed air past the nasal plug of his blowhole to emit a loud raucous yapping almost perfectly mimicking the creature's own racket.

Buster, the floppy-eared white, black-and-tan beagle furiously barking himself into a tizzy, suddenly stopped in mid-bark, uncertain whether to tuck his tail and run, or to stand his ground. In the time he had been a faithful watch-dock dog, he had never seen nor heard anything like this. A barking fish! Worst, the swear words the fish yapped sounded suspiciously like his own. Which of course was impossible. Dogs speak but fish can't. That, he knew for certain.

Striking a more defiant stance, the trusty dock-dog barked out some of his choicest swear words at the dogfish.

Head cocked as if listening, the dolphin fired them back just as smartly without missing a syllable. Buster stared at this gray long-nosed fish and wondered if he should go fetch his master. No, that might suggest he was unworthy of his watch duty. Instead, he finally acted completely indifferent.

He stopped bristling, loosened up, let his tongue loll out of the corner of his mouth and stared off in another direction. Out of the corner of his eye he saw the fish swim closer. Buster wanted to run, but his legs wouldn't move.

The dolphin executed a few fast rolls right under the dog, blowing a string of bubbles that burst behind him on the surface.

Buster acted as though he hadn't noticed. Mouth closed, nose up, he sniffed for a nonexistent scent. Then, quite aloofly, he stiff-legged his way slowly back along the dock, pausing at every other railing post to lift his leg and anoint it.

Trailing behind and below him in the water, the dolphin wondered at this weird ritual.

The seemingly indifferent watchdog jumped off the dock and walked up to the crest of a grassy knoll. Certain that he was in full view Buster decided to show off for this odd visitor. He started chasing his tail furiously. Around and around he went until he was nothing but a tan and white blur that spun dizzily off the crest to the other side of the hill entirely out of the dolphin's sight.

Fascinated, the dolphin turned back toward the bay, more convinced than ever that he had just seen one of man's more interesting creatures go stark raving mad.

At dawn the next morning the cool air, fragrant with the scent of pines and marshlands, was so still that sea birds, winging low over the bay on their way to the Gulf, clearly saw their reflections in its mirror surface. Suddenly, this pristine tranquility was shattered with a roar…a sound the dolphin had learned to love. It went, "…sput, sput, sputter…sput, sput, sputter-r-r-r-r-RRRRRRRRRRRRRRRRRRRARRRR…."

Instantly, the dolphin tore off swimming at top speed toward it. His heart pounded, his breathing quickened and the deliciously tingling sound waves sent titillating reverberations through him from head to tail. Not all of his kind reacted this way, but he loved the sound of an outboard motorboat starting up almost better than anything he could imagine. The mere thought sent shivers of delight through him.

Now, as the sound swelled to an underwater crescendo, he raced toward its source, almost drooling with unabashed excitement. His sonar picked up on the turbulence long in advance. Savoring the wave patterns with both mind and body, he surged through the water on that powerfully stimulating homing beam as if his life depended upon it.

It was a fishing boat with a large, powerful outboard motor running at full throttle. In a flash, the dolphin closed in on it. He shot straight for the source, the whirring propeller. Amidst the roar and the fury of churned bubbles, the dolphin performed a slow spin, holding his breath to maximize the joy he felt of turning around and around in the seething welter of tingling froth while every nerve in his body sent shock waves of pleasure coursing through every fiber of his being.

On across the bay went the boat and the shadow that seemed a permanent fixture to its wake. The man in the boat never saw what was chasing him, so intent was he on where he was going.

As the boat approached the opposite shore, the man throttled back. The dolphin did likewise, disappointed that the noisy whirler was slowing down just as he was getting warmed up.

As the man switched off the motor and reached for his casting rod, he heard, and then saw the dolphin. From the way the man's eyes widened as he jerked back and sent something crashing into the bottom of the boat, you'd have thought he saw a shark, thought the dolphin.

He porpoised around the boat impatiently, wondering how to make the whirler go again. The man was speaking and shaking his fist in the air.

"You blankety-blank," he shouted. "Scram before you scare off all the blankety-blank trout! G'won with ya. Git!"

The dolphin circled the boat warily. Something in the man's manner told the mammal that this was not an encounter of the friendliest kind.

Nevermind, he thought, it's the whirly that counts. While the man climbed into one end of the boat and began whipping at the water with a long, slender thing, the dolphin eased up to the other end and inspected the object of his adulation.

Tentatively, he fired a burst of high-frequency sound waves at it. The propeller just sat there. Drawing closer he gingerly nudged it with his snout. It moved but made no effort to spin.

No real mind of its own, that's clear to see, thought the dolphin as his sonar once again scanned the motor's entire lower unit. The mental image of cotter pin, gears, housing and a thick liquid more dense than water, completely baffled the dolphin. It looked like all the others he had ever seen. Just junk if it didn't move.

Come on whirly, he urged. Swim.

The propeller continued to just hang there glaring at him.

Maybe the boat made it whirl.

Drawing back the dolphin drove full force into the vessel's stern, punching it hard with the dome of his head the way he might a shark.

The boat leaped ahead, then sat bobbing feebly. The whirler failed to whirl. Momentarily out of sight until he picked himself off the bottom of the boat, the man just scowled, too mad for words. In frustration he hurled a boat cushion at the grinning dolphin. As it plopped some ways off, it received a quick scan to instantly identify it as more of man's junk. Then the mammal swam over, took the cushion's strap in his jaws and swam it swiftly around and around the boat until he was bored. Finally he carried it off and left it drifting some distance away. The last he saw of the man he was sitting down, holding his head and glaring at him.

The incident was already forgotten as the dolphin made his leisurely way back across the bay. All his memory bank did was play back the wonderful sensations he remembered from the deliciously wild and wonderful pursuit he had made behind the whirler.

The course of his wanderings brought him back once again to the dock where he had seen the crazy four-legged creature that had whirled itself right out of sight.

Lifting himself high out of water, he looked closely at the waterfront. The coast was clear. Not a living thing in sight. He heaved a sigh and let it trail off into the soothing sound of the fondly remembered outboard. Then, for no other reason than that he felt alone and lonely, the dolphin lifted his head and went, "Yappidy, yap, yap, yap, yap!"

From under an over-turned boat came a muffled, "Yip?"

A floppy-eared head popped up, then disappeared just as quickly. Something small moved swiftly through the tall saw grass along shore. The dolphin's heartbeat quickened. Buster broke through into view, his white-tipped tan tail straight up and wagging as if it had a spring in it; his ears up and on the alert as only a beagle's ears can be on the alert.

As Buster stood with all paws already in the water, his tongue lolled nonchalantly out the corner of his mouth while his nose and eyes sized up the situation. There's that crazy fish again that swears like a dog, he thought. Boy, he sure looks weird.

Buster walked a ways along the shore, high-stepping through the water; then he turned and walked back, watching the fish out of the corner of his eye. He wondered if he should lift his hind leg and leave his mark so there would be no question in the fish's mind about whose place this was. But somehow that seemed unnecessary. After all, it was only a fish. What do they know about canine customs and social amenities?

The dolphin, smiling broadly, cruised slowly up into the

shallows in front of the dog. Cautiously, they eyed each other. Seeing how big and brave the fish was, Buster bristled from head to tail. A low, menacing growl rumbled in his throat.

Ummm, that's a tough one, thought the dolphin. He tried to mimic it but it came out wrong, a little too high-pitched. But Buster was impressed.

Somewhere behind him a screen-door slammed. Without a glance to see if it was his owner, Buster sprang into action. Teeth bared, fur bristling, he jumped forward a few inches barking viciously.

Surprised, the dolphin recoiled in an explosion of water. Buster yipped and almost leaped backwards over his tail. Heart pounding, he risked a glance at the house. Nobody there.

Shame-faced, the hound looked back at the fish, whining a feeble apology. Ears up, fur down, tail wagging he was all friendly beagle again.

The dolphin took another chance on the crazy animal and moved closer. Buster kept his tail on full wag while bravely wading out until the water tickled his belly.

I don't know whether to trust this guy or not, he thought, racking his brain to remember what sharks looked like. He may be one of those that eat dogs.

The dolphin sent out a series of friendly clicks, bobbing his head and tossing amiable splashes toward the cautious canine.

Buster halfway persuaded himself that the thing was not a dog-eating shark after all. He had seen sharks brought in by deep-sea fishermen. The carcasses always got hung up for tourists to see and Buster had sniffed them out quite thoroughly. No shark he'd ever seen looked or sounded like this fish. For sure, sharks never smiled either. This guy had a funny long nose and a built in smile. Buster yawned to show how calm and cool he was.

In front of him the dolphin ya-ya-ed with his head and squealed out a perfect imitation of Buster's creaking yawn.

Then the denizen of the deep swam out into deeper water and playfully squirted a mouthful of water toward the beagle.

The invitation was unmistakable. Buster pushed off and swam out toward the waiting dolphin. He used his best beagle senses to size up the fish and from all the signs he read the fish wanted to be friends.

The dolphin was overjoyed to see that his coaxing had succeeded. He showed his appreciation by running through a repertoire of sounds, hoping to hit on maybe one or two of them that the dog would know.

Buster, swimming a leisure dog-paddle around the dolphin was taken aback by the sudden outpouring of sound. He cocked his head, perked his ears and listened, but all he could make out was a bunch of noise. It sounded like a combination of clicks, whistles, bird-chirps, quacking, barking, wailing and buzzing. Once or twice there was even the sound of a banjo. Buster decided his friend was talented all right but he sure talked funny.

Scanning the beagle with both high and low frequencies, the dolphin was dismayed to see how inadequately man's animal was made for water. He watched the four legs churning inefficiently through the water and saw at once what he needed – webbed feet. He studied the various internal parts of the beagle's anatomy with his fine-tuned sonar system, concluding that it was all very rudimentary. Still, he was a likeable creature.

Buster and the dolphin swam circles around each other, each of them gradually losing their fear of the other.

When the dolphin ducked underwater and swam around behind the beagle, Buster made a huge show of splashing vigorously back and forth while yapping at the top of his voice until the dolphin reappeared, ya-ya-ya-ing in response. Gradually their chasing and hide-and-go-seek turned into a friendly game of nudging and pawing; the dolphin doing much of the nudging with Buster using his paws whenever the dolphin allowed himself to be caught.

Whew! All this swimming was rough on Buster. I'm a beagle not a water spaniel, he thought. Wonder if this fish is any good at fetch.

Dog-tired but still game, man's best friend wearily paddled ashore. With gusto he shook himself off with a wave of vigorous twitching and twisting coursing from the end of his wet nose to the tip of his spotted tail. Water flew every which way to the delight of the dolphin.

After that, Buster sneezed a couple times and grabbed a sizable piece of driftwood off the shore. Momentarily he was tempted to run in the hope of being chased. Then he remembered about his legless companion and lunged back into the water again, the driftwood clenched in his teeth.

The dolphin chirped happily, pleased to see that they were still going to play. What exactly it was they were to play was as yet a mystery to the dolphin but he was game to learn.

Buster swam around him with the driftwood held high out of water, a growl rumbling in his throat.

The dolphin scanned the object and immediately knew what it was and how dense it was. Is this a gift, the dolphin wondered? He was pleased if it was.

Buster kept swimming rings around the slightly perplexed sea creature. When he realized that the fish wasn't going to try and take it away from him as he had hoped, he did what always worked with a human. He swam up, dropped it right in front of his companion, then backed off and barked. Under the circumstance's Buster's bark came out sounding more like a wet sneeze.

Instinctively the marine mammal grabbed the driftwood with his mouth and flipped it over his head into the bay.

With a fit of hacking and yapping, Buster almost popped his collar struggling to get to it. When he finally did, he snatched it up and swam it back to the dolphin, dropping it inches from the end of his nose.

Once was all he needed. The dolphin understood immediately. While he thought it a simple kind of amusement, he went along with it to humor his floppy-eared friend.

Once again the dolphin picked up the driftwood and hurled it some distance away. And once again Buster broke all canine dog-paddling records capturing it and returning it to the dolphin.

The mammal emitted a burst of complimentary clicks that ended in a soulful sigh. Simple pleasures for simple creatures. But he threw the stick again for the hassling hound and watched him struggling through the water toward it.

Instead of waiting until the dog got it, however, the dolphin held back just as long as he could, then he streaked to the stick and snapped it up an instant before the beagle's jaws clamped on it.

Buster yapped and heaved an inner sigh of relief. Dog-gone if he ever thought this character was going to get the hang of the game. Great swimmer, reflected the beagle, but he sure is stupid.

The dolphin did a slow backstroke toward shore, moving just enough to keep ahead of the loudly splashing and bow-wowing Buster. The pooch loved it.

Both the dog and dolphin buddies kept up some kind of game the rest of the afternoon, the dolphin constantly varying their activities to avoid getting bored. In or out of the water Buster was beside himself. He hadn't had so much fun since the day he chased a family of skunks out from under the house and they perfumed him for it. For his effort his Master saw that he spent the rest of the week living outdoors in his dog coop getting aired out.

Carried away with the good time he was having, the carefree canine should have known that the slammed screen-door he had heard earlier was significant. Though they had seen no one, the dog and the dolphin were being watched intently from around the corner of the boathouse.

# Grits'n'Grunts

Up the sandy hill from the boathouse, facing both the bay and the Gulf of Mexico, the tired, gray, weather-beaten house vaguely resembled a long forgotten mansion someone with tastes had built there. But one could see it had spent too many years exposed to sun, wind and ocean mists. Though flanked by equally weathered sand pines, their green presence failed to conceal the fact that this once magnificent house had long since passed the point of no return. Where it had earlier stood proudly crowning the pine covered sand ridge, it now sagged sadly in disrepair, a weary caricature of its former self.

Despite its dilapidated condition, the house fitted in with its surroundings. It tilted and rambled with the terrain. Its crooked lightning rods, bent weathervane and angled gables whose shake shingle roof bristled with old pine straw, seemed a part of the surrounding pine trees. Even the spacious wrap-around veranda with its ripped screen and paint-flecked rockingchairs, matched the setting. The entire house was dusted with the same pale green patina of pine pollen and salt mist of age that afflicted the whole area. Everything was just plain old.

At a kitchen window looking west toward the sea, as a young woman hung up her apron her dark eyes lingered for a moment on the golden sunset. Then, glancing down at her little sister who had just helped wipe the dishes, she said, "Better call Buster to supper, Bonnie."

"Okay." Off came the oversized apron as she tossed it toward the cupboard and with a flash of yellow pigtails, ran to open the back door.

**"Bus-ter…Bus-ter…Here Buster, come get your Kibbles'n'Bits!"**

Lea marveled that so much sound could come from such a tiny person.

"Bonnie, why do you always do that?"

Wide-eyed the family's youngest looked back at her willowy sister.

"Do what?"

"Give the neighborhood the dog-food commercial."

"Ohhh, it ain't for them. It's for Buster. He might not come if I said grits'n'grunts. Yuk!" Bonnie wrinkled her nose.

Lea shook her head. "Bonnie, Buster likes grits and grunts. Just like we do. He was raised on them."

"Double yuk," said Bonnie.

An almost waterlogged beagle shot through the open door and skidded to a halt on the slippery linoleum.

"Oh! He's soaking wet. Take him outside and let him shake off." Lea tossed a towel over the shivering dog. "Give him a rub-down too."

Buster groaned inwardly as the little mistress collared him through the towel and skidded him across the floor and out the door. Might know, he grumbled. Call me to supper then run me off. Then he brightened at the thought: Maybe it's something special tonight!

Lea got Buster's bowl from under the sink. She fingered the teeth marks in the plastic. Amazing. Buster may be getting more nourishment out of his bowl than his food.

At the stove she carefully spooned in a generous helping of still warm grits. Then she carefully flaked meat off the bones of the small fried fish left on a paper napkin and sprinkled them on the bowl of porridge.

"Kibbles'n'Bits, Kibbles'n'Bits …We're gonna get some Kibbles'n'Bits…" came the sing-song voice as Bonnie and Buster burst through the door and ran excitedly around the kitchen, the faithful watch-hound yapping excitedly with the giggling Bonnie, the dog doubly stimulated by the rubdown and the possibility of the forthcoming feast.

Lea placed his bowl on a newspaper in the corner. Buster took one look and stifled his jubilation. When I'm dead and gone, he reflected darkly, they can put on my tombstone: Here lies ol' Grits'n'Grunts, done in by one bowl too much of the stuff. The beagle hungrily attacked his supper.

Bonnie skipped out of the room as the door yawned open, then slammed shut, rattling the dishes in the cupboard as another Holloway entered.

Lea winched.

"Hey! Where's Grandpa?" asked the boy who was already head and shoulders taller than his little sister. Lea's tow-headed little brother stared wide-eyed back at her. Hair messed up, shirt unbuttoned, jeans grimy. The usual disaster area.

"Livingroom, I guess. Working on his net."

"Thanks, Sis." Brother Gregory's wheels spun, trying for traction as he started to roar toward the front of the house.

"HEY!"

Gregory slammed on brakes. "What?"

"You eaten?"

"Naw. I don't like Kibbles'n'Bits."

Buster looked up from his food bowl, ready to offer some of his.

"Who caught the grunts?" asked Gregory.

"Grandpa. Off the dock early this morning."

"Great," said the boy, grabbing a bag of potato chips off the kitchen table. "These'll do."

Before Lea could object, her brother's tennis shoes squealed on the linoleum and he blurred out of her sight through the door into the dining room and was gone.

Lea rolled her eyes. "Oh, brother…" she murmured.

Holloway House's living room was more like the main salon of an ocean liner from another time long gone by. Spacious was the word for it. Heavy beamed ceilings stood high above their heads. Between the doors or windows that opened onto the veranda, walls were covered with memorabilia of a lifetime spent at sea. Framed charts, pictures of sailing ships, floats, starfish, an old harpoon and several stuffed fish collected dust there.

Several low hatch-cover tables and massive chairs with deep overstuffed cushions sat here and there. The epoxy-coated hatch cover tables placed in strategic spots supported more souvenirs of the sea – three different sized model sailboats, and a classic steamboat, their riggings hoary with accumulated dust; a scrimshaw-carved walrus tooth won in a poker game, four black hand-sized fossil shark teeth, one broken in half, while three table lamps ingeniously made from driftwood when lit illuminated the collection of artifacts.

The original collector of these things sat hunched under a big brass cabin lantern that had been wired for electricity. In its glow the old man's fingers deftly worked the carved wood shuttle that fashioned the mesh of the huge nylon cast net draped over his lap.

"Gramps!" Gregory shouted, as he burst into the room, "I saw Buster playing with a big fish by the dock!"

"Take him outside and hose him down before your sister smells him," muttered the old man around the stem of his pipe without looking up.

"Not that kind of fish." The boy crammed a fistful of potato chips into his mouth and munched nosily. "He wasn't rolling on a dead fish or nothin'. He was in the water with him."

"Least he kept clean," said the old man.

"They were playing together," repeated Gregory. "Like kids. I watched them from behind the boat house after school," Gramps looked up frowning. "You weren't sneaking a puff, were you?"

"Awww, Gramps. I'm just a kid."

"Huh. These days you never know."

The white-haired old man in the paint-splattered faded blue denims turned back to his net.

"It was big," continued Gregory between fistfuls of chips. "Looked like a porpoise fish."

Gramps looked up and took his pipe from his mouth.

"A porpoise is a dolphin but not a fish. He's a mammal. There is a fish called a dolphin but this isn't him. This dolphin breathes air just like you and me."

"Oh-h-h yeah-h-h." Gregory dimly remembered hearing that before.

Grandpa studied the youngster for a moment, seeing him quite clearly but getting flashes of a big baby sparrow, all mouth, consuming endless handfuls of potato chips.

In the kitchen Buster laid on a rug in his corner chewing his empty plastic bowl and daydreaming he was gnawing a steak bone.

Gregory's older brother Chip, a lanky youth with blue eyes and curly brown hair, sat at the kitchen table downing some cold pizza pie while he told his sisters about the shark attack, "Harry swears it's true. Said the shark slammed into the boat and knocked him right off his feet."

"Where was that?" Gregory asked, wide-eyed.

"Right here in the bay. Harry was fishing for trout near the inlet when it happened,"

"Wow! You gonna try and catch him?"

"You bet," said Chip. "Larry and I been talking about putting out a shark rig from the point near the pass. Water drops off pretty good there. He might be hanging around it."

"Can I go too?" Gregory asked. "I'll help pull him in."

"Well-I-I-don't…"

"Hey, I almost forgot. …Guess what I saw Buster doing today!"

"Chasing his tail?" asked Bonnie.

Gregory shot her a dark look. "No. He was playing with a dolphin."

"What?" said Lea glancing up from patching a pair of Gregory's jeans. Everyone else was suddenly listening too. Gregory paused, savoring the moment.

"Uh-huh. Near the dock, close to shore."

"Sure it wasn't a shark?" Chip smirked.

"No, honest. It was a dolphin. They were in the water swimming around together."

"Boy, that's weird," said Bonnie.

"Oh, I don't know…" Gregory slid his chair closer to Chip, eyeing his pizza. "You see it on television sometimes."

"Yeah, but they're trained to do that." Chip let his brother steal a wedge of the cold pizza. "I never seen no dog and a dolphin before."

"Maybe it escaped from a zoo," Bonnie snitched a corner of Gregory's booty before it was inhaled.

"Dolphins don't live in a zoo, dummy," Gregory corrected, "they live in quariums."

"Well…whatever."

"Maybe he's a wild one that just got friendly," suggested Lea.

"All I can say is Buster better be careful about who he messes around with if there's a shark in the bay," said Chip.

The faithful household guardian's ears pricked up at the mention of his name, but he was largely gone from reality, dreaming a fantasy about chasing cats with a loudly barking buddy that looked like a big gray fish.

## Eye-Spy-In-The-Sky

Nothing about Holloway House was more intriguing than its ATTIC. It was a world unto itself. While it took in a large part of the rambling structure – the part closest to heaven in some of its inhabitant's minds – it was as apart from the house as you might say a treehouse is apart from planet earth.

The narrow door to The Attic stairs was in one corner of Grandma's bedroom, the one upstairs room in the house that almost no one but Gramps went into. It was intended, but rarely used, as a guest bedroom. Gramps said Lea always kept it as neat as a pin, whatever that old saying meant. Gramps got it from Grandma for sure.

To Bonnie and Gregory everything in the bedroom from its small four-poster walnut bed covered in a colorful patchwork quilt to the tiny dressing table and footstool was Grandma. It looked like her and it smelled faintly of her powder. But that went only to the door in the corner.

Open that and with one step you were in the world of The Attic. It began as soon as you opened the door and switched on the faint yellow light coming, dully from somewhere far above and beyond. The door was always opened and closed quickly, and then you started up the steep, creaking unfinished wood stairs smelling the smell that only old attics have. If the boxes and bags stacked in the corners of the stairway were not enough of a clue, the smell of old things that strongly permeated the place was evidence enough that this was indeed, The Attic. At the top the stairway you looked left and you were there. What your eyes saw was a sight that had to be beheld to be believed.

The roof's bare pine boards and timbers sloped and slanted in every imaginable direction. Or so it seemed. There were only two pointed-top windows. One at each end of The Attic. Both were cob-webby inside and salt-encrusted outside.

Stacked from one end to the other in this great rambling wood vault was every conceivable kind of thing from the past – hat racks, big round-topped wood chests, and trunks; stacks and racks of old stiffly starched clothes, boxes galore of cardboard and wood; old worn out toys; a doll's house with tiny porcelain dishes, cups and even miniature silverware; baskets within baskets; old games; a collection of old picture frames and boxes of old saved postcards with strange stamps from all over the world; boxes of old Kodak snapshots of people in old clothes that no one knew but kept anyway; jigsaw puzzles in fancy cardboard boxes with pretty pictures on them; old box cameras; big heavy colored horse-shoes for some kind of yard game where men tossed the things at iron posts in the ground; some wooden balls with mallets and wire loops falling out of a box whose tattered paper label in bright colors declared it to be a game called Croquet; old long forgotten broken radios, stacks of phonograph records and record players from a long ago time.

Under the sloping roof's rafters were fishing rods, nets, a folding table, several shotguns and two rifles, tennis rackets, felt school pennants plus a long board with a six-foot-long dried and scale-flecked hide of a diamondback rattlesnake nailed to it. And that was just a smattering of the treasures.

At the moment, however, Gregory who had Bonnie in tow was more interested in dragging the long brass tripod-mounted telescope out from behind a tall rusty bird cage on a paint-chipped red and blue stand.

"But why?" asked Bonnie. "Why do we need that old thing?"

"*Hon*-nestly, Bonnie, sometimes you ask the stupidest questions right after I explain something to you."

"I *know*, Greg-gory…I know what you said, but why can't we spy on Buster from the yard?"

Gregory groaned, almost falling over the birdcage stand as he tried to disengage one stubborn tripod leg from something that had it caught. "We can't do it there, silly. Buster's no dumb dog. He'd catch us sure."

"Oh well, all right," Bonnie sighed, helping her brother grip the stubborn leg and drag it the rest of the way, along with an ancient Venetian blind that clattered and spilled out all over the floor like something that had come alive.

"Wow!" gasped Gregory. "Kick that monster back while I set this thing up."

Bonnie kicked vigorously until the blinds clattered reluctantly back into their lair. Gregory dragged his find off, struggling with his awkward burden while the tripod took every opportunity to thrust its legs into nooks and crannies in an attempt to hang on.

With sheer determination, however, the boy won out, managing to drag his tarnished relic through an obstacle course of Attic treasures to a wooden ladder. The ladder led straight up to a trapdoor in the roof. Since the roof was low, the ladder was short, but not short enough that both Gregory and the telescope could negotiate it. So he set it up at the bottom of the ladder, spreading the tripod's legs so the telescope could stand by itself. Which it gladly did since it had been leaning against the birdcage with its feet tangled in the Venetian blind for at least the last three years since the boy last took it out.

Gingerly, Gregory climbed the short distance to the roof and pushed up. The hinged door groaned but it opened and folded back on the roof outside. Gregory climbed out onto the flat platform built over the peak of the roof and reached down. "Okay, hand it up to me."

Bonnie wrestled the legs of the telescope out of their comfortable resting position and teetering, lifted the whole thing the few inches to her brother's outstretched hand. Then it went with him up and through the open hole in the roof onto the six-foot-square platform built there surrounded by a sturdy wood balustrade of a railing about waist high.

Once the way was clear, Bonnie scrambled up the ladder after her brother. They now stood on this enclosed flat section of rooftop whose railing and wood floor were deeply cracked with age and bore only a faint trace of the white paint that once covered them.

This was the Widows Walk, a place that afforded a grand view of both the bay and an impressive sweep of the Gulf of Mexico. Many of the real old houses along the coast used to be built with them. It was where the wives of the seamen went to watch for their husbands' boats coming in from the sea. It was where Grandma Holloway always came on stormy nights in her raincoat to watch for Gramps piloting the old *Tarpon* on its freight runs from Pensacola to Panama City.

The children all knew the story of the *Tarpon*; how Gramps always blew the boat's loud steam whistle each time they steamed past Forb's Inlet until the night of the big storm. Caught with too much heavy cargo in her hold, the creaky old boat sprung a leak and was going down. But Gramps kept her together long enough to make it back as close, as he could to the inlet before the storm simply tore the steamer apart.

He and all but one crewman made it ashore. Gramps always said the only light on the whole coast that black stormy night, the one light that he steered for, was Grandma's big brass kerosene lantern she had hung from the Widows Walk so Gramps would have a light to find his way home.

One seaman drowned but the others washed ashore hardly a hundred yards from the inlet. And it was Grandma who alerted the local fishermen so that they were on the beach ready to help them.

Gregory had the telescope's tripod in position and the long brass instrument focused on the end of the dock when he saw Buster come trotting into view. The boy could tell he had something important on his mind because the hound was moving briskly along using his no nonsense trot.

Most beagles employ this gait when they have pressing engagements. It is a tail up, curved forward like a periscope trot while the body moves ahead on an angle, head pointing forward, ears up and alert, tongue out in a casual lolling manner from the down-wind corner of his mouth. To any but the most astute observers of beagle body language, Buster was the picture of canine nonchalance out for a stroll. But for those who knew better, such as the watchful Gregory, Buster was a study of dogged curiosity and exuberance held in check by perfect control.

"Boy, he's good," murmured the boy admiringly as he followed his canine's casual but unerring trot toward the far end of the wooden dock.

"Let me see, let me see the tell-scope!" begged Bonnie.

"Okay." Gregory hoisted his little sister up and she squinted through the telescope's eyepiece.

"See him?" Gregory grunted.

"Uh-huh."

"Well – what's he doing?"

"Pee-peeing on Mr. Rose's tackle box."

"Huh?" Gregory dropped his sister like a sack of sand. Quickly he glued his own eye to the telescope. "Oh…my… God!" he breathed.

"**Greg**-gory!" admonished his little sister. She aimed a kick at his shin but all it got was a grunt.

"Jeeze…he did…all over it!"

"Mr. Rose'll be mad," decided Bonnie. "Bet he won't leave it alone again."

Gregory moved the long telescope up and down but saw no sign of the big burly bait man. But he was sure he was somewhere close by because his casting rod leaned against the dock railing just a few feet away from the closed metal tackle box.

"Whew…that took real guts." The boy stared admiringly after the briskly trotting beagle nearing the end of the dock.

Buster now trotted with a little extra spring in his step. Courage had nothing to do with what he had just done. It was pure canine cunning.

Canine cunning was an everyday thing for Buster. He had passed the shuffling burly bait man by a wide margin minutes earlier on the way to the dock. The man in baggy, begrimed overalls had stopped and cast a squinty bloodshot glare at Buster as the dog came into focus for him. But the tackle box on the dock was too much temptation to resist. In Buster's sometimes oddball reasoning, it relieved something in his Inner Self. And besides, it couldn't have happened to a more deserving fellow.

Today was an incredibly fine Saturday morning. Day like this every dog in the world had to be at peace with life. Buster stood on the upwind corner of the T-shaped dock with his head under the lower rail and sampled the air. His keen beagle nose told him that somewhere up the beach a large dead fish was ripening in the sun. The aroma had all the ingredients to give a really discriminating dog that smell of distinction.

Buster considered beating his way upwind for a fast roll in it but on second thought he remembered the consequences of his last such indiscretion. The faithful watch-beagle was banned from the household for two days; then Chip had the dubious honor of giving him a thorough washing in the bay with half a bottle of Lea's bubblebath. After that he smelled so flowery the only dog in the neighborhood that would have anything to do with him was the Broward's hound dog, Smut. And that was only because he was so old he couldn't smell anything anymore.

Buster's nose merely noted the delicious aroma in passing while his keen beagle eyes swept the glittering surface of the bay for a familiar form. Somewhere out there was that crazy fish that talked like a dog. Buster wondered if he would ever come again.

Seeing nothing but a lot of glittering water and a couple

distant fishing boats, Buster decided to lie down and wait, his head resting out over the edge of the dock where he would miss nothing. Narrowing his eyes to the reflected glare of the water, he began his vigil, his wet nose twitching occasionally as he whiffed the far off forbidden fragrance that could make every female dog for miles around sit up and take notice of him.

Bonnie tugged on her brother's shirttail. "Greg-gory, Buster's fallen asleep."

"Naw, he's just watching."

"How do you know? You can't see his eyes."

"Oh, I know," Gregory assured her. "Buster sleeps curled up. When you see him like that, with his nose pointing between his paws, that's his watchdog position. He uses it all the time when he's on guard, like now."

"Hmmm," said Bonnie, momentarily satisfied. "After what he did to Mr. Rose's tackle box, he might better turn around and keep watch the other way."

Gregory failed to hear her comment. The telescope and his attention were now focused on a distant fishing boat that was acting funny. The motorboat was spinning around in tight circles. Gregory frowned and tried focusing better. Even at that distance he knew who was in the boat. It was the old maid Phimple sisters. He recognized them by the funny big pink sunbonnets they always wore fishing. Grandpa said they called them Mother Hubbards. It had something to do with a saying about Mother Hubbard's Cupboard. Anyway, they always fished in them.

But they weren't fishing now. They were crouched down in their boat and flying around in circles, their big bright pink Hubbards turned almost inside-out from their speed.

Gregory and his sister took turns watching their strange circling antics until finally the outboard sputtered to a halt. The sisters in their inside-out sunbonnets were seen suddenly beating at the water with the boat's oars.

"Good golly," whispered Gregory in awe. "They must

have got sun-stroked."

*"Let me see, let me see,"* Bonnie begged, never having seen anybody sun-stroked before.

Gregory boosted her to the eyepiece. She studied them long and hard. "It's that shark after…"

Bam! He dropped her!

**"Greg**-gory! **You nitwit!"** screeched Bonnie as she picked herself up and aimed another kick at her brother's shin, but this time it didn't even get a grunt. The tell-scope had him.

He was glued to its eyepiece, the long brass scope instantly nailed on the distant action. So engrossed was he in what he saw that he never heard his little sister march off in a huff.

Bonnie clomped down the ladder, thoroughly disgusted with her nitwit brother. Flouncing past a dusty cardboard box of toys near the head of The Attic stairs, she snatched up a half undressed doll with a missing arm and just one blue glass eye. The other one was flipped backwards showing funny wires and things. Tucking the unfortunate under her arm, Bonnie tromped on down the stairs, mollified by the knowledge that the dolly was going to be a lot safer to play with than her ugly brother.

Meanwhile, back at his post on the Widow's Walk, The Nitwit was almost beside himself with excitement. At first, when he saw that something big was swirling the water around the Phimple sisters' boat he knew he was going to see a huge man-eating shark leap out of the water and do its thing right there. His heart pounded, his eyes watered, the darn telescope kept going in and out of focus, and the eyepiece got all steamy.

"Now **cut it out!"** he yelled at himself. He tried holding his breath to calm himself but that only made him pant. Finally, despite all his shaking and sweating, he slowly began to realize that what he thought he was seeing was something completely different.

That realization came with his sharper focus on the

96

"shark" in question. The curved dorsal fin and loping runs of the "attacking" fish looked strangely familiar. When at last the shark lunged head and shoulders out of water in front of the cowering Pfimple sisters doing its ya-ya-ing gestures, the boy knew at once it was Buster's friend, the dolphin.

Although they may have understood the difference by then, the Pfimple sisters were taking no chances. All Gregory could see of them now were the tops of their sunbonnets as they crouched in the boat. Then, an arm and an oar appeared at the back of the boat. The oar was plunged into the water, worked vigorously back and forth and the boat wobbled off.

Gregory was relieved to see them sculling for shore. But what about the dolphin? He retrained his telescope.

No longer interested in a boat whose whirler no longer whirled and showered him with oceans of tingling bubbles to tickle his dome, the dolphin now had another playmate in mind – one that wouldn't try to hit him over the head; one that didn't even know what an oar was.

Racing his shadow across the shallow sandbars and mud flats of the bay, swooping high to briefly skim the surface before swooping down at top speed through the amber depths again, the dolphin came up with a mental picture of the four-legged, floppy-eared land animal he had romped with the day before. The mere thought of the awkward creature with its skinny tail, thrashing spindly legs and ungentle voice, made the dolphin grin broader than usual. He knew the animal was not made for the water world. But this was one of the animal's most likable traits – his courage. At least he tried, and that pleased the dolphin a great deal. Were it possible for the dolphin to come ashore and play in his world, he doubted that he would be half as brave and not nearly as able.

From atop the Widows Walk, Gregory was starting to get excited again. The dolphin's speedy course had not gone unseen. The boy was tracking it with the telescope so accurately it was as if he were electronically locked on the target. In his growing excitement, however, he kept steaming the scoped eyepiece.

"Wowee!" he exclaimed. "Look at that guy come!"

"Yap-yap-yap-yap-yap!" barked Buster excitedly. His dogged determination not to fall asleep but to keep his vigil finally paid off with what he now saw cleaving through the sun-glittery water.

Up and on his feet, pert tail waving, ears alert, he had difficulty restraining his excitement. The closer the hurtling shape came, the wilder Buster's tail fanned the air. Occasionally, he voiced an excited yap, but mostly he kept himself under control, eagerly whining under his breath while his paws tap-danced on the planks.

When the overjoyed beagle was sure his buddy was heading for the dock, he turned and started high-tailing it back along the dock toward shore.

Suddenly, in the middle of the dock, tromping toward him like a freight train taking up the whole track was a scowling, red-eyed Larry Rose, a foaming can of beer clutched in one massive paw, a six-pack in the other.

Though there was plenty of room for them to pass each other, Buster was appalled to see the burly bait man stop, puff up, spread his arms and legs wide, and go into a gorilla crouch blocking his way as he called, "Here doggy, doggy," leering like an evil dog-catcher.

The fast-trotting beagle slacked his speed not one iota. But in seconds he changed from being a nice little hound dog into a hunkered down something quite different. Nose pointed bullet-like; tail down and streamlined, fur up and bristling, ears back, head low, teeth bared, he shifted into high gear and was no longer a mild-mannered beagle but was now a pit bull of flying fury, a blood-curdling growl thundering in his throat.

Larry Rose just had time to focus his blood-shot eyes on what was coming at him on a collision course before he dropped everything and leaped for his life. A tan and white streak scorched past the very spot where he stood a second before, and was gone in a clatter of flying beer cans before the dizzy bait man peeled himself off the railing wondering if he had really seen what he thought he had seen, or whether it was something he had just imagined.

Still a bit whack-o from the experience, he stared at his overboard beers gone to the bottom and beyond reach, then he staggered over, collected his rod and tackle box and started to walk off the dock. Suddenly he stopped and put down his fishing gear. Muttering darkly to himself he wiped off his hand on his overalls and wondered when it had rained.

# Oy...Oy...Oyyyyy

From his lookout atop the house, Gregory saw it all. He was scared seeing Buster cornered and threatened when he couldn't help. But when his mild-mannered beagle faced up to the situation as he did, tears of pride welled up in the boy's eyes.

Totally awed, he thought, **He's Superdog**! Equally impressive was the beagle's swift change back into his customary role of his usually friendly, perky, inoffensive self.

Whew! Smoother than Superman to Clark Kent, marveled Gregory, again following the now jaunty Buster as he bounded down the beach to a grassy point and splashed out to meet his bright-eyed, broadly grinning yap-yapping friend. Buster knew now that noise was a dolphin laughing.

Gregory stayed with the telescope just long enough to make sure the two were playing together. Then he grabbed up the tripod and wrestled it back down through the trapdoor.

With one hand he closed the roof and clattered down the ladder. The tripod's legs poked frantically at everything to keep from falling. Gregory unscrambled them from between the ladder rungs then pushed the whole contraption into a rack of old clothes. The tarnished old instrument collapsed gratefully among the soft, frilly, lavender-scented ladieswear of a bygone era.

Racing through The Attic, Gregory, for some reason, snatched up an old, curled brass taxi horn. "Honk!" it squawked as he squeezed its rubber bulb to test it. Satisfied, he clamped it under his arm and clumped swiftly down The Attic stairs two at a time. Bonnie was at the kitchen table serving her one-eyed doll a cup of tea and a sugar cookie when her brother burst into the room with a horn honk.

"Go get on your bathing-suit," he yelled. "We'll play with Buster's dolphin."

"What's the horn for?" asked Bonnie.

"To call him," Gregory shouted over his shoulder as he bee-lined for his bedroom on the back porch to find his swimming trunks.

Bonnie wiped the loose sugar off her dolly's face and left the nibbled cookie beside the two cups of tea for later.

From the junk-crammed confines of Gregory's closet came her brother's muffled voice. "Where's Lea and Chip?"

"Lea's gone for groceries with Gramps," shouted Bonnie. "I think Chip and somebody went shark fishing." She paused, reflecting on her big brother's news the night before.

"Greg-gory!"

"Huh?"

"You sure Buster's friend ain't that shark?"

"Sure I'm sure." Gregory appeared in a pair of ragged cutoffs that looked as if Buster might have chewed on them. "I know a dolphin when I see one and that fish's a dolphin."

"A mammo," corrected his sister.

"Yeah, mammal. Go get your suit on, Smarty."

"Okay." Bonnie bounced off toward her room, taking her one-armed tea guest with her.

Waiting impatiently, Gregory saw the sugar cookie on the kitchen table an instant before it disappeared. Tea didn't interest him. He practiced his honking.

Bonnie finally came out wearing her daisy suit, the faded yellow petals of summers past definitely drooping the bloom. But holding them all together around her waist was an inflated green-and-white-spotted froggie float with red eyes glaring at the world.

"Jeeze," said Gregory. I hope you don't scare him off in that outfit."

"Oh, don't be a pill," said the daisy frog as it prissed by him and bounced out the door. Gregory squeezed off one more agonizing squawk of the taxi horn; then hurried to get ahead of his weird little sister.

In the water beyond the point the dog and the dolphin tumbled and rolled in good-natured play. Buster especially liked their game of hide-and-seek. When Buster turned his back, his slippery buddy ducked. Then Buster charged back where he should have been, pawing water like mad while his hindquarters did a furious dog paddle. Here and there he went, watching for bubbles, whining excitedly when he saw the shadows shift, then suddenly the yapping fish erupted in a surge of water where he was least expected. Buster bow-wowed his joy and the dolphin chattered with equal delight.

Sometimes the game took the form of rather rough and tumble tag. When Buster was doing the chasing, the dolphin swam purposely in circles but on his back, just out of reach of the eager beagle, but then when Buster turned and feigned indifference, the dolphin would come close and the dog would "tag" him with flaying forepaws.

Then it was Buster's turn to flee while the dolphin chased, making believe he had trouble swimming, letting Buster lunge almost out of water onto shore before he reached out and grabbed the end of the beagle's tail, "tagging" him to a standstill. Back came Buster, lunging after the seemingly indifferent but tantalizingly just out-of-reach-dolphin.

It was during this activity that Gregory and Bonnie crept through the tall sawgrass on the point and quietly slipped into the water.

The dolphin spotted them long before they were in the water. As they entered the water he scanned them with his sonar, uncertain whether retreat was the best policy or whether they were no danger to him.

To be on the safe side he left the beagle and moved farther out beyond the drop-off where he doubted they would come.

What's wrong with him? wondered Buster. He barked at the dolphin at the same time he yapped excitedly toward his young masters.

Bonnie, still not absolutely sure that her brother or Buster knew the difference between a shark and a dolphin, stayed near shore. But Gregory swam out to the faithful family protector and spoke low to him.

"Who is your friend, Buster?"

The beagle whined a reply as best he could. Gregory, treading water furtively studied the sleek gray form that slipped in and out of the surface some distance away. Boy! He's big! He thought. His heart was thudding in his chest. He half wished he were sitting sanely beside his sister at the water's edge instead of out here where he couldn't touch bottom and that big thing could get him if it really wanted him.

That thought made the boy move in a ways where his feet finally touched bottom. At least knowing that something wouldn't come up unseen under him was some assurance. The dolphin, meanwhile, beamed a series of high-speed click trains at both children. The reflected signals of his echo ranging revealed quite unimpressive information.

Like the four-legged animal, these two-legged young ones were equally ill-adapted to his world. But they were air breathers like him. He had checked them inside and out, examining their curious lung capacity and the strange arrangement of the organs. The littlest one in particular interested him. She was different. Unlike the one in the water that acted more aggressive, she was built with a much larger lung capacity; a kind of fish bladder appendage in her middle that was her froggie float. That one surely could not even get under water, reasoned the dolphin. The creature would always have to float on the surface, totally dependent on the whimsical winds to move it about, much as did the purple and pink stinging bladders of the sea. Was this young one also capable of stinging? Even fine-tuning his sonar he detected nothing bad, but the dolphin decided that one bore watching. Buster, growing tired of the pause in their play, dog-paddled ashore and managed to stir up some response when he stood directly behind Bonnie to shake.

With a squeal, the little mistress popped Buster a good one, then leap-frogged in to rinse off.

*Clickety-clickety-clickety*, with the speed of light, almost, the dolphin's hunch was verified. That one was a floater. No stingers. But the other one was getting closer, bubbling and making air sounds. The dolphin cautiously exposed his upper head and blowhole, listening.

"C'mon boy," I won't hurt you," Gregory burbled more to himself than to the dolphin. "Come here, boy. Let me pet you."

Same gibberish they always speak thought the dolphin. Slow, awkward noises. Worse than those made by the four-legged creature. If they were able to communicate even the most rudimentary information with their crude low-frequency sounds, it would surprise him. But somehow their own kind understood them.

"C'mon boy," soothed Gregory, getting closer than he really meant to that big shiny dome of a head with its broad grin and shiny eyes.

The dolphin tossed his head and opened his toothy jaws, warning the youngster that he had come close enough. At the same time he had a try at mimicking the strange sounds he was making, " - *oy... oy... oyyyyy*," said the dolphin.

Wow! What teeth! Gregory stared at the evenly spaced bullet-pointed white ivories big as the first joint of his finger.

"Come away!" cried Bonnie near shore. "You're making him mad. He'll eat you!"

From his look inside the dolphin's mouth, Gregory shared some of his sister's fear.

Trying not to disturb the big thing any more than necessary, the boy turned and eased himself toward shore.

"*Ooy...oy...oyyyyyy*," sounded the bottlenose, tossing his head.

Eyes wide, Gregory moved into the shallows beside his sister.

"Did you hear that Bonnie?" her brother blurted out excitedly. He said, "Boy…boy…boy! He's calling me!"

"Sure he is," said Bonnie. "He wants to eat you."

"Oh, will you shush?" Gregory grabbed the taxi horn and waded out into waist deep water. Buster splashed out behind him, filled with canine curiosity. Gregory thrust the brass bell of the horn underwater and squeezed the rubber bulb.

"Ssqquua-a-w-k-a-burble-burble," came the muffled gurgling of the horn, making a sound that was shockingly unfamiliar to it in a place that was totally alien.

Unlike the boy who felt the dull vibrations against his leg and the dog whose ears instantly pricked up, the dolphin to his amazement received a far more forceful response.

The raucous sound traveling five times faster underwater than in air affected him more rapturously than ambrosia to a Greek God or catnip to a cat. Brief as it was, the titillating sound waves were of just the right frequency and pitch to tickle his whole sensing system.

"*Again! Again!*" the dolphin replied loudly in Dolphinese. "*Do it again!*"

As if responding to the request, the boy blasted away with the horn underwater.

Bonnie wrinkled her nose at the unbecoming sound. Buster barked since it seemed like the most sensible thing to do.

The dolphin did a slow roll, luxuriating in the waves of sound flowing around him. Slowly he swam toward the tantalizing source.

Gregory saw him coming. He didn't know whether to stay or run. Buster's barking only made him more nervous. Bonnie had already scampered ashore wearing her froggie float and now stood high and dry, admonishing her brother for his foolishness.

But Gregory couldn't stop once he started. His hands were frozen to the horn. He pushed it as far out in front of him as possible and just stood there like an idiot, squawking it.

Tingling all over from the sound that was almost as delicious as that made by the' boat whirlers the dolphin approached to what would be called in any language, point blank range. His snout almost touched the dull brass horn bell beaming out its strangely sensuous massage to this creature from another world.

Underwater the bottlenose scanned this marvelous contraption and marveled at its cunning simplicity. Thrusting his head out of water he emitted an "-*oy...oy...oyyyy.*"

"That's it, that's it," encouraged Gregory, squeezing the horn for all his worth. "Say, boy, say boy!"

"-*oy..oy...a-oy..a-oy...*" responded the dolphin, nuzzling the bell of the horn.

"Good! Good!" exalted the boy. Without thinking, he reached out and patted the dolphin's glistening dome. "Gee, it feels like rubber!"

The dolphin drew back, unsure whether he dare allow this kind of familiarity. The touch was not hard but soft as the underbelly of a mullet. Really, rather soothing.

"You be careful Greg-gory," beseeched Bonnie from the safety of the shore where she clutched her froggie and was glad it wasn't *her* hand that was so close to those horrid looking teeth.

"I think he likes me," said Gregory. "He let me touch him."

Buster couldn't stand it any longer. Dogs get petted not fish. He blundered forward, pushing his head between the boy and the dolphin, eagerly seeking some petting of his own.

"**Bus**-ter! Get out of here! You'll scare him off."

With his best hangdog look, the family defender paddled to one side. He knew when he wasn't wanted.

The dolphin rolled sideways, dipped under and came up behind Buster to tug playfully on his tail. "Yap, yap, yap!" barked the dolphin.

Buster barked a jubilant reply and lunged for the mischievous looking fish that was so good at echoing him.

The two drifted off in a furious rolling, tumbling, and splashing display of exuberance that impressed both children.

Gregory waded ashore and sat down with his sister, grumbling under his breath that Buster had messed up everything.

"Don't worry," said Bonnie, "just be glad he didn't bite you."

A shrill whippoorwill whistle sounded. Gregory glanced over his shoulder. "*Oh nooo!*" he groaned.

Three boys his age had just dropped their bicycles in the grass and where loping toward them. "Hey, Greg. We thought a shark had you sure."

The speaker was Freddy Dumshek whose father owned the inlet's only fish market. He had red hair, dime-sized freckles to match and an impressive mouthful of shiny tooth braces.

The other two were Harvey Clemens, a thin, sandy-haired boy who always, had a fishy smell about him since he worked in the Dumshek's market, mostly cleaning fish. The other was Joey McGumphy, a kid with a usually dripping nose, curly brown hair; wearing thick glasses in front of squinty eyes.

"Hey, what is with your crazy dog?" asked Harvey as they came up, the boy radiating the aroma of Dumshek's Market.

Gregory stepped upwind of him. "Awww, he's just playing with a dolphin," as if it were something Buster did everyday of his life.

"Playing pretty rough," said Freddy, bubbles of spittle lurking around the rubber bands that held his braces in place. McGumphy squinted through his thick glasses at the spectacle. "How long's this been going on?" he sniffed.

"He always does it," put in Bonnie, finally relaxing her grip on her froggie. "He does it all the time,"

"Awww, I just started," said Gregory. "I saw it the first time yesterday. But he let me pet him!"

"That's nothing," Freddy Dumshek shielded his eyes and

stared at the two cavorting beasts. "I've seen that on television lots."

"Not with no wild dolphin, you haven't," said Gregory. "Those were trained. This one ain't."

"And he's got terribly big teeth too," put in Bonnie.

"I'm not afraid of him," said Dumshek.

"Me neither," piped up Harvey the odiferous.

"Or me," added McGumphy.

Gregory looked at his companions. He knew he couldn't keep the dolphin secret. Not now. By Monday it would be all over school.

"Okay," he said. "If you be real careful and not scare him, you can get in the water and play with him."

"Sure...why not?"

Dumshek had already turned and started for their bikes.

"We'll get our suits," he said.

Later that afternoon, as Gramps and Lea turned off the highway just before the bridge and rattle-banged the old pickup along the pot-holed clay road toward the docks, they saw the commotion near the water's edge. "What the devil's going on?" Gramps wanted to know.

"Pull off here and let's see."

"The boys are just swimming, Grandpa."

"I can see that, Lea. What I can't make out is what that is they're playing with. Looks like a big fish."

Lea. looked more carefully. Her hand flew to her mouth. "It is, Grandpa. It's that dolphin Gregory was talking about. You don't suppose he can hurt them?"

"No, not likely," said Grandpa. "If anybody'll need help after that bunch gets through with it, it'll be the dolphin. Let's go."

# Har-har-har-har-r-r-r-r....

Gregory was right. By Monday afternoon every kid in Forb's High School knew there was a wild but friendly dolphin in the bay. And that afternoon, after school, half of them roamed along the east shore near the docks, looking for him. But the dolphin did not appear.

At the time, he was on the other side of the bay, carefully herding a school of mullet toward a narrow pocket. Once the fish crowded into the corner where he wanted them, the bottlenose swept in for the attack, snatching them left and right with his powerful jaws. Only after eating his fill did he cease his efforts. The remainder of the panicky school spilled past him out into the open safety of the bay. The dolphin, no longer hungry, cruised on up the coast past great stands of pines, looking for amusement.

Suddenly, his far-ranging echo locating senses picked up a familiar form, one the dolphin was surprised to find in the bay. Could he be wrong? His heart beat faster; he speeded up, diving deeper to scan the bottom depths of the gloomy bay.

There it was again, moving slowly just ahead of him. It was a big one. The dolphin angled obliquely away from the shape, then cut back to approach from its side where he would have a more direct attack course if it became necessary. The ultrasonic signals were bouncing back to him much more rapidly now as he closed with the form. Then, in the dim brown gloom, he saw its ugly, heavy-bodied, undulating shape.

The bull shark paid no attention to the dolphin. The broad-headed creature had no sophisticated sonar to tell him the dolphin was near, but his many sensing pores that literally covered his head and body, alerted him to his presence. Those receptors along his sinewy flanks that man called the lateralis line, had felt the pressure charges in the water long before he appeared. Sensors around his head and gaping mouth picked up the dolphin's electrical field, identifying him.

Both animals felt and evaluated the other's presence.

They were not friendly, but they were not combative enemies either. Both passed, and went their way, the shark sluggishly moving along the mud bottom searching for flounder, the dolphin making a mental note to be more wary. The bay was not as safe as it once was.

The shark's presence in brackish water was not unusual to the dolphin. Had it been one of the great ocean sharks that would have been unusual. But this was one of the sharks that could adapt itself to a mixture of fresh and salt water, which made it especially dangerous to all creatures. It could come and go at will between the Gulf and the bay. The dolphin would have felt better if it was simply gone.

The month of May brought an influx of fishermen to the bay. They came to rent boats and catch a variety of both fresh-water and saltwater fish that lived in the bay. It was a time of boundless activity around Forb's Inlet, the year's peak time to be making money from the visiting tourists. Cottages were rented by anglers from Florida, Georgia and Alabama, all converging on the inlet and its adjoining large body of water. Most came seeking the fat speckled trout, fleet fish with tender mouths that hooks often pulled free from, making them not the easiest fish to catch. For that reason, "weakfish" was the name they bore on other coasts, but here they were simply "specks," fish great to catch and even better to eat. The baitmen, boatmen, dockmen, tacklemen, and fishermen of this small coastal community on the Gulf of Mexico owed their livelihood to the abundant schools of speckled trout that twice a year in the spring and the fall blessed Forb's Inlet.

For the dolphin, all this activity was more fun than he could ever have imagined. Powerboats, rowboats, outboards galore, they all became his most stimulating toys. Their whirlers turned at a variety of speeds and sounds that were almost more pleasure than a dolphin could stand. Wherever their spinners spun and their bubbly wakes foamed the brackish waters, the dolphin found it all but impossible to keep himself from homing in on the source. Once there he swam like a dolphin possessed, nose to spinner, his shuddering body luxuriating in the tingling sensations that were more fun than he could ever imagine.

What confused him however, were the mixed responses he got from the people in the boats. Some – especially those with their young – seemed genuinely pleased to see him racing behind in their wakes. They shouted and waved and encouraged him the same way the children and the dog had done when he played with them near shore. He knew by their sounds and their expressions that they enjoyed his antics. He saw these same expressions of delight in most of the speeding boats he pursued across the length and the breadth of the bay.

The confusion came when the boats stopped. This was the part he could never understand. Once they stopped and he bumped them with his head to make them go again, the people changed their expressions toward him. Instead of waving and laughing they now frowned and shook their fists. Though the dolphin was not too good at understanding much of their sign language, he knew that certain motions and facial grimaces meant joy and acceptance, while other signals meant just the opposite.

While the spinners go and they make the roaring and bubbling, everyone likes me, he reasoned. But once the spinners stop and the things all come to rest on the water, they suddenly dislike me. Though he understood what was happening, the dolphin could not help but believe he could persuade them to like him again if the spinners would just spin again. So he often persisted…persisted to the point of sometimes bumping the spinner so hard from in front that it sometimes knocked the thing high out of water. Yet other times when he hit them, the things never went up; they stayed down and the boat jerked backward from his blow. Those times seemed particularly upsetting to those in the boats.

This action always brought signs of extreme anger and dislike from the boaters. It was particularly noticeable when the dolphin chanced upon an anchored boatful of fishermen. His bumping brought him nothing but trouble. Old ladies flayed at him with long cane poles while old men tried to hit him over the head with their boat's oars. Some threw pop cans in his direction while others flung their boat cushions at him. Still others simply shook their fists and shouted epitaphs that he was glad he did not understand.

Despite all the abuse he took, the dolphin could no more avoid chasing outboards than he could fly. With the coming of summer his reputation as a chaser and a bumper nearly excelled his reputation as a performer. Now he appeared almost daily near the grassy point where crowds of children came to play with him. Under the pines up the hill the crowd of spectators from all over grew ever larger, people hardly believing that an untrained dolphin was doing all the tricks he did.

"It's so...so unnatural," some of them said. But to the dolphin it was the most natural thing in the world, playing in the water with his two-legged and four-legged friends. The latter came not so much because of their masters' urging but because Buster had passed the word around the canine community that the big fish that could bark like a dog was more fun than a barrelful of cats on the run.

Daily the dolphin learned more about his human admirers. His apprehension in their presence was long forgotten. While he not always understood their strange pattern of play with him, he quickly picked up basic tricks and responses that just came naturally to him. They rewarded him with much clapping and laughter. This was all he cared for. That and the pure joy of the whirlers.

One fine summer day a photographer from the *Gulf City*

*News* came to take pictures of the dolphin playing with the children. Addis Walker, the inlet's honorary mayor passed the word that he wanted a good turnout. "Any publicity we can get out here is better than none," he said. "Even if it is just about a dolphin."

The kids came, the dolphin appeared and the photographer went to work. Standing unsteadily in a speedboat, the lanky longhaired man wearing jeans with a camera in hand ran the show.

"Six of you kids come out here where I am and pet the dolphin," he said.

Gregory and a bunch of youngsters his age broke away from the crowd on the beach and waded out into waist deep water.

"Hold it! Everybody doesn't need to come." The reporter motioned back an onslaught of eager actors. "I want you in the background watching it."

The photographer looked through his camera. "You with the horn," he motioned to Gregory. "What's that for?"

"He likes it when I honk."

"Okay, okay. Do it. The rest of you kids sort of move in close to him. Get the dolphin between you."

Gregory held the bell of the horn in the water and squeezed the rubber bulb. The squawk was almost inaudible to the reporter but he saw the instant response from the dolphin that had been waiting in the wings, so to speak, wondering when someone would get in the water and start playing.

The instant he heard the familiar sound, he loped in, swam around the group of children on his back, then rolled up and gave Gregory's noisemaker a nudge with his snout.

"That's it! That's it," enthused the photographer, clicking away with his camera. "Now pet him."

A halfdozen hands reached out and patted the dolphin's flanks.

"Awwwwwwwrrrr," he responded.

"Here's his ball, Bonnie shouted from shore, holding aloft a brightly colored plastic beach ball.

"Yeah…Great, kid. Somebody toss it out for her." The photographer's eye hardly left his camera. His camera's motor drive purred, and he kept shooting, verticals, horizontals, high ones, low ones, he didn't miss a trick.

The ball skimmed close enough for beefy Forb's High football star Larry Rose to make a spectacular flying lunge for it.

"Okay. What's he do with the ball?" asked the photographer.

"He goes for the big bomb," yelled Larry Rose, grinning wide for crowd and camera.

"All right, let's see it."

The boy's fist punched the ball into a highflying arc that carried it far out over the water. Everyone watching its long lofty flight missed seeing the water boil around the youngsters.

What they saw was the light plastic ball dropping gently toward the water when suddenly the dolphin shot out directly beneath it like a Polaris missile, caught it deftly on the tip of his snout and punched it back toward the children. The audience of bystanders yelled and clapped their approval.

"Man, that's pretty good," said the photographer. "You sure he hasn't been trained?" he asked suspiciously.

"Swear it, Man," yelled Larry Rose, center stage again as he wrested the ball away from Freddie Dumshek who was going to give it to him anyway. "He learned it on his own. I throw him passes all the time like that. Keeps me in practice." He grinned for camera and crowd again.

But the photographer already had the shot he wanted. Now he wanted a close-up of the dolphin.

"Hey kid," he called to Larry. "How about seeing if you can lift the dolphin out of the water so I can get a shot of you and him together?"

"Sure," beamed Larry, showing off the missing front tooth

he lost in last season's playoff. "Hit the squawker, Greg."

Gregory honked the horn.

Dutifully, the dolphin swam up between them and laid on his side, nuzzling the object whose voice reminded him of a lovesick female he once knew long ago.

The beefy quarterback edged closer. Then, seeing his chance, he bent down, clamped both arms around the dolphin's midsection and tried to straighten up.

All he got was the big dolphin's head and forequarters out of water briefly before he lost his grip. The dolphin fell in with a great splash.

The others may have missed it but from his high vantage spot the photographer saw almost as if in slow motion what happened next. As the dolphin fell back into the water, he started to leave. Then, almost as if on second thought, he backed up, and swatted Larry Rose in the seat of his pants with his tail. Then he dashed off in a wild, tail-walking, head-bobbing noisy display of mimicking that went *Har-har-har-har-har-r-r-r-r....* ending on something that sounded strangely like a raucous raspberry.

"Well I'll be..." said the photographer.

After that the photographer's speedboat operator fired up the powerful outboard and boatman, cameraman and dolphin roared off across the bay, the photographer still clicking away at the torpedoing gray form that stitched the frothing wake directly behind the roaring engine.

Through the spatter and spume, the photographer's practiced eye saw it all in stop-action scenes, the movement slowed to a fraction of its actual pace. Through his camera lens the photographer zoomed in on details – the dolphin's almost ecstatically glazed eyes, the broad shiny dome of his head showing the vivid cuts, scrapes and scars of previous joyous encounters of the very closest kind with that lovely whirling thing.

"Wow!" marveled the cameraman to himself as his Nikon clicked it all in rapid-fire sequence recording the lone dolphin's battle-scars he got for his love affair with an outboard motor propeller.

On shore, most of the crowd was breaking up. The excitement was over for a while. Only a few youngsters stayed to ogle Larry Rose's rapidly reddening behind.

The beefy boy strained to look at his rear. "Jeeze, I thought he bit me!" the football star moaned.

## S/V *Fantome*

Lea, the oldest daughter of the Holloway family was not only the quietest one but also the one who in her twenty-two years had been the most adventuresome. Like her grandfather who thought she was surely an angel come to live with them, her father had followed the sea.

Since he was a sea captain who believed in keeping his small family with him, she had the good fortune of spending her childhood living on the small island of Bimini in the Bahamas. Her father, Captain Randy Holloway was the much-liked skipper of a trading vessel known throughout the Bahamas as "The Sugar Ship." That was her name: *Sugar*. She was a 300-foot steel-hulled sailing ship from the past that carried trade goods throughout the islands. Mainly that was sugar but anything that was needed or could be traded went along as cargo too.

Home-based in Bimini, Lea got to make many trips with her father through the islands. Everyone knew and delighted in seeing the lithe young girl with the flowing jet-black hair that she tamed by wearing in a tight poneytail out the back of her white billed hat. When she walked, it bounced saucily. She was a pretty girl with piercing dark eyes that looked directly at a person, always with a hint of a smile on her lips. Lea took to the crystal clear blue Bahamas waters like one of their own. And of course she was exactly that because she had grown up in all of its tropical beauty of sun, sea and sand. She not only swam like a fish but learned from other Bahamian youngsters the secret of free-diving and the ability to hold one's breath for extremely long times. She was a natural free-diver. She never forgot the exciting sailing trips she made with her father.

Nor did she ever forgot the stories her mother read to her when she was very young. They often were about little girls who learned to talk to the animals. Lea loved the thought of being able to do that. When she was a young teen-ager she learned that there was a marine research facility on Bimini that was experimenting with the possibility of teaching bottlenose dolphins to understand our language.

The man in charge of this facility was a scientist who spoke with an accent. It was said that he was carrying on some research with dolphins in connection with a study being made in those years by the U. S. Navy. His name was Dr. Emile Reinhart.

Typical of the Holloway trait of stepping right up and going after whatever goal they were interested in, Lea showed up at Dr. Reinhart's laboratory one day and said she heard that he was working with dolphins. She said she was interested in his research and offered her services for free if she could be part of it.

Completely charmed and bemused by this young woman's offer, Dr. Reinhart invited her to tour his dolphin research center with him. He introduced her to his assistants and did the same introductions with her to the three dolphins he was presently working with. Their names were Henry, a young male dolphin, Ruby, an older very loud talking female dolphin and Sissy, a younger female. Quite obviously, right from their first meeting, Lea saw that Ruby ruled the roost over the other two.

Afterward he told her he would like for her to come back and just write down her observations of what the dolphins did while he worked with them. And as she left he gave her a book to read. He had not written it but he said the author described the work he and other scientists were doing in this field. The book was titled, *Secret Languages of the Sea*.

Within days Lea had read the book from cover to cover. She was fascinated not just with the details about dolphins but by the many ways underwater creatures had of communicating with each other. They had languages all their own. The first time we became aware of this was during World War II when the navy put underwater listening devices along our East Coast with the intention of picking up the sounds of enemy submarines. Surprisingly, listeners recording these sounds heard a cacophony of noises coming from underwater creatures communicating with one another in ways we had no idea ever existed. One of the few species that never made any noise was called flashlight fish. These fish winked messages to others by luminous pouches under their eyes!

Talk about weird, thought Lea but all of it fascinated her, especially when it told how dolphins communicated together using a click language in frequencies that sometimes were out of our hearing range but when they sought to mimic or "talk" to humans they did it not only in our frequency range but by shaping their sounds more like our words through their blowholes atop their heads where they breathed!

In a chapter titled *Communicating with Dolphins* Lea was especially fascinated by a description of experiences one researcher had and how impressed he was when he realized a dolphin was imitating his words and repeating them back to him. It detailed the experience of a Malcolm Brenner of Sarasota, Florida trying to teach a pet dolphin to say his name. Here is what she read:

> **Spotting Ruby's ball near the pool**
> **Brenner decided it was a good opportunity**
> **to use Ruby's fondness for a game of catch**
> **as a reward to see if he could get her to**
> **mimic her name. He threw the ball to her**
> **and she quickly threw it back. They did**
> **this several times. The dolphin was**
> **enjoying the interchange enormously.**
> **Then Brenner withheld the ball and said,**
> **"Come on Ruby, say Rooo-beee, like that.**
> **Come on, you can do it. Say Rooo-beee."**

Instead, Ruby squeaked Dolphinese in reply to Brenner.

"No, no," Brenner said. "That's not it. Say Rooo-beee." He held up the ball, withholding the reward.

As he continued urging her to pronounce her name, he suddenly became aware that her squawks had changed considerably. The sound was now distinctly two syllables. Nothing significant except that the two syllables were sounding strangely like those he had just been repeating for her. In response and as a reward for this, Brenner threw the cherished ball to the dolphin. In minutes he realized that she was beginning to copy the same speech pattern that he was using, even to the inflections of his voice, to mimic the very word he had been saying – "Rooo-beee."

Brenner was amazed that she had picked it up so quickly. Each time her pronunciation seemed less like his, he withheld the ball. Whenever Ruby replied with a sound that more closely imitated her name, he responded with the ball reward. He said, "We stood a few feet apart in the water of her pen, staring at each other intently with bright eyes and the excitement between us was palpable. Never in my life had I known such an intimate feeling of being in contact with an incredibly nonhuman creature. It felt like it was what I had been created to do. Our minds seemed to be running on the same wave. We were together.

What astonished Brenner most was that all of this had happened in less than ten minutes!

That was fascinating information to Lea. She had heard her little brother telling them how he got the wild dolphin to mimic his repeated word, "Boy." So that's the name Gregory gave him.

In the next few months she helped Dr. Reinhart with his efforts to communicate with his dolphins, but he had only marginal success.

Now, so many years later, everything had changed for their family. When Dr. Reinhart passed away so did interest in that line of research. A hurricane drove her father's ship *Sugar* onto the shallow Little Bahamas Bank and tore her to pieces. The U.S. Coast Guard saved the crew who escaped with their lives before the grounded ship was totally destroyed by the storm. Scattered over hundreds of feet of white sand bottom in a mere sixteen feet of water its metal parts now became a habitat for sea creatures. It made one of the finest shipwreck dive sites in the Bahamas, especially at night when every sea creature there sought it as a place of refuge. Scuba divers loved it when their dive boats brought them from Florida to dive it because at that depth a diver's air seemed to last forever.

Since her father was nearing retirement age, losing their only means of livelihood was a terrible blow. But when considered from another angle her father thought maybe it would turn out for the best. After all he was nearing retirement age. This might be the time to do it; to retire from the sea. The insurance payment for their losses from the shipwreck would last them a lifetime. So the decision was made and the whole family moved to his old family home in northwest Florida's Forb's Inlet where her Grandfather welcomed them with open arms.

Lea graduated from Florida State University with a degree in Marine Biology and took a job with the U.S. Naval Diving and Salvage Training Center at Panama City not far from Forb's Inlet. Their research was no longer with dolphins. Now she worked with naval research scientists on diver problems. Currently she recorded monitors a diver wore in a water-filled room with glass walls where he rapidly pedaled a stationary bicycle in near freezing water. The navy wanted to know how much a diver without a wetsuit could endure before giving in to the cold water.

Lea often thought of her parents and wished they were all back together in the Bahamas as they had been when she was young.

"Why oh why did they do it?" she often asked when she remembered the terrible events that took both of her parents from them.

Her father was a friend of a young ship captain who sailed the Caribbean in one of the last large sailing ships of its kind. The great ship's only reason for being was to take tourists and Tall Ship lovers on cruises through the warm tropical seas where they could all re-live the kind of adventure these great ships once provided.

Since her parents had never celebrated their retirement, they decided to do so by accepting the young skipper's invitation. They would join him for his last cruise of the season sailing this tall ship through the Caribbean. It would be a fitting final hurrah for the times that would never come again.

The whole family was excited about them going. The name of that sailing ship was *Fantome*.

In late October 1998, with the Holloways aboard, the 679-ton staysail schooner *Fantome* sailed out of the harbor at Honduras on a six day cruise through the islands. At the time Hurricane Mitch was over 1,000 miles away, expected to possibly threaten Jamaica and the Yucatan Peninsula. To be safe the ship's captain decided to sail for the Bay Islands and take cover until the storm passed.

But the following day Hurricane Mitch changed course. *Fantome* immediately changed course and sailed for Belize City where it disembarked all of her passengers and non-essential crewmembers. Captain Holloway and his wife Ella stayed aboard believing they might be of some assistance to their friends.

The schooner then left Belize City heading north toward the Gulf of Mexico. When word was radioed to the sailing ship that the storm would most likely hit the Yucatan before the ship could get out of harm's way, her skipper changed course and headed south. It was too early then to know that she was heading directly into the storm's path.

The sailing ship planned to head for the lee side of the island of Roatan in the Bay Islands in case Mitch made landfall at Yucatan or Belize. They figured this island would protect them from the high winds and large swells.

By this time the hurricane was a Category 5 with winds up to 180 miles per hour. As the storm moved in on Roatan and Honduras, *Fantome* made one desperate attempt to flee to safety heading east along the backside of Roatan toward the Caribbean. But the storm's forward motion abruptly increased and the *Fantome* was unable to outrun the storm. The ship and her crew were never seen again.

In a last radio message she was fighting 100-mph winds in 40-foot seas. They were just 40 miles south of Mitch's eye wall. Shortly after that radio contact was lost with the *Fantome*.

A month later, a helicopter dispatched from a British destroyer discovered the life rafts and vests labeled "*S/V Fantome*" off the eastern coast of Guanaja, the island just to the east of Roatan in the Bay Islands. This was all that was ever found of the vessel. All 31 people aboard perished. With them were Captain Holloway and Ella. This tragic news hit the Holloway family hard.

Now, Lea and her Grandfather took care of the entire family. At least they were all together and happy. What she had been hearing about the wild dolphin that had shown up in the inlet interested her. She always loved dolphins and their playfulness. Now that this dolphin was relating to the dog and kids, Lea was eager to meet him too.

But she didn't want to make a big thing of it. She

especially picked early one Saturday morning while the rest of the family were asleep. She left a note for them.

The soft green of Lea's two-piece bathing suit blended nicely with the deep tan of her willowy figure. Pushing her long black hair back over her shoulders, she picked up her yellow net dive bag containing her mask, fins and snorkel.

As Lea slipped out the door, she also carried the only other thing needed – the magical brass taxi horn that Gregory said was the best dolphin caller in the world. Wisely he had attached a plastic float so it would float with its bell underwater. He had also added a line so it could be carried easily over a shoulder.

# Laaayy-aaaahhh

As a rosy sunrise glowed brighter across the eastern horizon Lea walked along the narrow white finger of sand that led to Sandy Point. Well beyond their dock the point dropped off quickly into the aqua marine colored bay water. It was where Lea always beached her white 10-foot Zodiac Cadet inflatable boat. Under its blue tarp it sat well above the tide line at the end of the point. She loved the boat because it was light and fast with its 15-horse Evinrude.

Sandy Point was Lea's favorite swimming spot. The water was always clearer here than in other parts of the bay. Probably because it was closer to the mouth of the inlet and got plenty of clear incoming tidal waters. She stepped into the shallows. The water was just cool enough to be refreshing.

Shading her eyes Lea looked out across the bay hoping to see the dolphin frolicking somewhere out there. But she saw no sign of him. Possibly he was out of hearing for the taxi horn. But since it was Saturday, when the local kids always sought him out for playtime, maybe he wasn't too far away. She took her gear out of the bag and tossed it ashore.

Rinsing her mask in the water, she put it on, adjusted her snorkel and moved out into the deeper water where she slipped on her swim fins. Then she pushed off face down to watch the bottom.

Below her a pale flounder exploded out of the sand and disappeared over the edge of the drop-off. Smoothly using her fins, Lea swam straight out for a while enjoying the feel of the water and the flexing of her strong leg muscles. She swam smoothly with her arms at her side, the dolphin-caller riding more on her hip where its drag was less noticeable.

In the Bahamas Lea had learned, as all long-time divers learn, that the moment they enter the water they automatically slow their breathing. It is a scuba diving habit to conserve air. She did it now as she moved quietly, swiftly and smoothly out across the surface of the bay.

This was her world. She always felt at home once she was there. She held back now from her desire to slip beneath its cold embrace and dive spiraling down into the emerald depths savoring every wonderful sense of at last being back in her silent world of the sea with everything it had to offer her. The experience was always almost mesmerizing for her. Lea knew why dolphins always seemed so happy. Who wouldn't be in this beautiful liquid world they lived in?

Only when she was well away from shore did she pause to swing the horn around and with the rubber bulb out of water she squeezed off a few blasts. To her ears its raucous sound seemed far away but underwater she knew it was much louder.

Sounds are magnified for us underwater and seem to come from all directions. In the Bahamas she used to scuba dive for lobsters along the sides of boat channels. Most divers overlooked them there in their eagerness to search for them in the offshore reefs. That was their mistake. For that reason boat channel lobsters were often overlooked. Scuba was a necessity there because you had to stay down.

When powerboats passed near her in the channels the sounds of their motors were deafening and she often had to clutch the bottom weeds and turn her head to one side to avoid what sounded as though the thundering roar and the spinning propellers were right atop her. But they were always a safe ways away.

Again Lea paused to look across the glittering surface for signs of her rolling wild dolphin but she still saw nothing. Just as she put her face back into the water and her eyes adjusted to the green darkness below her she saw a school of small mullet racing under her heading in the opposite direction as if something was chasing them.

Thinking maybe the dolphin was coming, she let the rubber bulb of the horn fill with air then she surface-dived straight down into the deep green below her and squeezed the bulb.

Now she heard it much louder, just one raucous squawk of low-frequency pulsed sound. And it was at that instant that Lea's years of underwater experiences coupled with what she had learned at University and what she was doing suddenly struck her.

Whether it was because she first saw and felt the massive movement of water just beyond her or what it was, she later couldn't remember. But she emitted a long throaty "AAAwwww noooo!…" and stopped squeezing the horn because just now she remembered that low frequency pulsed sound underwater not only attracted porpoises but it was long known by scientists to be the one thing that most quickly attracts sharks like a dinner bell.

Even as she headed up she wasn't prepared for the sight of the bull-shark's broad brown head emerging from that green darkness below her and coming straight toward her, homing in on that powerful sound that in his world meant a creature in distress.

Lea knew this from growing up with sharks in the Bahamas. She also knew that bull sharks could be trouble. They were a sneaky breed, often attacking without warning. The only real enemies they might have were other sharks in competition with them for food. Lea was in his territory and had called him to her. Now, whatever was going to happen was up to him. And he was a big one, about nine feet long. How could she have been so forgetful? Living on a brackish bay you forget those dangers. No other sharks were ever a problem in the bay.

As she rose to the surface she watched him slowly circling her. Was he just curious and sizing her up? She knew what signs of aggression to look for. As they turned together she always faced him. If he threatened her some sharks would drop their pectoral fins, stiffen their body and arch their back. It was their warning. But bulls sometimes never warned; they just attacked.

She saw none of these signs. She kept the brass horn between them in her left hand. Her right hand she kept doubled in a tight fist with her thumb facing forward. It was her most lethal weapon. The single most important organ to a shark are his eyes. If his head is involved in anything a protective membrane covers his eyes automatically, protecting them. When a great white comes in for a bite, he rolls his eyes back into his head. Lea knew that on rare occasions some shark attack victims with their entire head and upper body in the jaws of an attacking shark who were able to have their arm free could reach around and jab their thumb into the attacker's eye. That act alone saved their lives when the shark quickly spit them out.

But before it got to that, all Lea remembered later was feeling a tremendous rush of water beside her, then glimpsing a huge gray moving shape that rushed past her like a battering ram to slam deeply into the side of the surprised bull shark, knocking it completely away from Lea.

*It was the dolphin!*

She was so stunned that when she looked where the shark had been all she saw was the grinning excited face of Boy bobbing his head at her and making all kinds of excited whistles, clicks and other strange noises!

She had no idea what happened to the bull shark. Lea was so sorry it happened. She had been to blame for calling him to her. Now she hoped that he had not been too badly injured.

Lea knew that dolphins and sharks coexisted together only when they left each other alone. Dolphins had no menacing teeth like those of a shark. But their large, dome-shaped heads made deadly weapons. A blow like she just saw delivered to the body of a shark was enough to rupture vital organs and end their lives.

But now all she could think of was this dolphin's highly inquisitive face in front of her. His eyes were locked on hers while his powerful sonar clicks swiftly scanned and evaluated everything about her. In an instant this uncanny sea creature knew everything about her both inside and out.

On the surface Lea held up her hand palm flat toward the dolphin, took her snorkel out of her mouth and slowly enunciating her syllables to the watching dolphin, she said, "Helll-loooh, Boooyyyy!" And she repeated it.

On the surface the dolphin bobbed his head as he studied her and the sounds he emitted from his blowhole remarkably were two-syllable and sounded to her like, "aaahhlo oi-oi-boi…." He repeated it over and over, each time saying it clearer.

Lea responded by vigorously nodding yes and clapping her hands. The dolphin seemed to grin even more with his mouth wide open also nodding yes with his head while the sounds he made sounded to her like dolphin laughter.

The dolphin was indeed laughing but the sounds he vocalized by manipulating the lip of his blowhole was his mimicking of Buster's happy barking. "Yap, yap, yap," made all the more humorous with his wide-open grin.

Lea closed her flattened hand and pointed at herself. "Laaaayyy-ahhh…. Layyyyy- ahhh."

The dolphin cocked his head; his eyes danced, "aaayyy-ahhh…yap, yap, yap…aaay-lay-ah."

"*Yes, Yes*! "Lea nodded her head vigorously and repeated it all again. By the third time he repeated her name perfectly and she vigorously made all the signs indicating how happy she was with his saying it correctly.

Then she pointed to him and said, "Boiiii…Boiiii," then pointed at herself and said, "Laaayy-aaaahhh."

While she had his eager attention, Lea pointed toward Sandy Point and her house and put her fingertips together so her fingers formed the point and her arms formed slants like a roof. "Hooooooommmmmmeee" she said. The dolphin had no trouble mimicking this sound but she was unsure that he understood what it meant. She tried it another way.

While Boy watched her every move he saw her spread her arms far apart as she said, Booooiiii hooooommmmmmeee,"and then pointed both arms toward the Gulf of Mexico.

After repeating this several times he seemed to understand. At least he did a lot of nodding yes with his head. Lea was amazed how quickly he caught on. All the time the dolphin was checking her out with his underwater clicking sonar and his eyes.

She wondered why Boy kept looking at her knees, especially the backs of them. Why? She wondered if the connection might be because that was the general location on her of the female dolphin's genital slit. He knew from his scan that she was female. Now he might wonder where it was! If that was it, she shook her head and laughed, thinking, Boys will be boys, no matter what species they are. Mother Nature saw to that.

At first the dolphin was a little shy about letting her get too close to him but as they swam together and he began mirroring her every move, this feeling of shyness quickly left him to be replaced by the fun of the moment.

Lea knew that the dolphin was extremely interested in her. It gave her a strange feeling. He knew more about her that she knew about herself. His eyes were what affected her the most. Come to think of it, these mammals were the only ones whose eyes seemed to show recognition and feelings. No one would ever see any hint of emotion in the eyes of sharks. They just stared. Their eyes were always blank and cold. But the eyes of a dolphin were so different. She saw humor, feeling and intelligence there. She knew she wasn't the only one that saw that either. Dr. Reinhart and all his researchers were well aware of it. And their mentor, Dr. Lilly, who always believed that any animal that had a brain larger than a human brain, as bottle-nose dolphins have, they *had* to be smarter than we gave them credit for being. He said there was something strange in the way dolphins made you feel when you became aware of this. Lea remembered that Dr. Lilly described it as a "feeling of weirdness;" that one was in the presence of a powerful intellect waiting just the other side of a barrier that you were trying to penetrate because on the other side was someone or something trying just as hard to break through that barrier to reach you.

Lea certainly felt that now. From this Boy's eager responses her pupil was ready and eager to break down that barrier right now!

She didn't want to push too hard. She wanted their meeting to be fun. Lea took a breath and surface-dived to the bottom, slowly spinning around as she went. One look at what she was doing and Boy was slowly turning that way right beside her. Breaking surface with just her snorkel for a quick breath he did the same as his blowhole sucked in a lungful and as Lea went into a graceful forward somersault underwater he too did it, then it was Boy's turn to show off.

He performed a perfect backward somersault and she did too, this time they came up facing each other as Lea reached out and gripped his flippers. When they reached the surface, Boy went onto his back and she was on the surface and instead of breaking contact he speeded up swimming backwards as she held on tightly to his flippers taking her on a high-speed rush through the water.

After that they both paused to catch their breath. Then he backed up to her and she realized he was offering her his dorsal fin to grip. Using both hands she took hold of it and he gave her a high-speed run around in a circle that she could not believe how fast he went. After that the two of them came together upright in the water and Lea embraced Boy. They couldn't be more together. With that he grinned and pushed his snout up to her and she took the hint and kissed him on his chin. After that he leaped out of the water beside her and did a lot of yap, yap, yapping. She made him feel young again and Lea couldn't be happier.

# Troubled Waters

I first heard about the wild dolphin that came into Forb's Inlet from my fishing buddy, George Brown. George was a retired railroad man and a cousin on my mother's side. George built his home near Sunnyside Beach just a short distance to the east of the inlet and since I lived in north Florida I often drove down to fish with him. George was a fishing buddy of Captain Holloway's and all the kids loved him.

George nicknamed the wild dolphin Nudgy because of his habit of pushing boats so they would run for him. Once they powered up the dolphin became addicted to the thrill he got in their wakes. George invited me down one day to photograph all the Holloway kids and their dog playing with the dolphin they called "Boy." It was a beautiful summer day and everyone was having fun. I stood on the end of their dock and got some fine shots of the dolphin playing with Lea, Gregory, Buster, and Bonnie.

The dolphin was on his best behavior. On cue from a suddenly started outboard motor, he shot across the intervening water to hover in a state of almost unrestrained excitement behind the idling motor, as if daring it to go. When it was slipped into gear, the boat leaped away with the dolphin seemingly glued by the end of its snout to the spinning propeller. Around and around they went in tight circles until the motorboat sputtered to a stop. With an adroit lift of his head, the dolphin tipped the foot of the motor out of water and a crowd of bystanders in the shade of the pines on shore applauded.

Gregory honked his taxi horn underwater and the

dolphin streaked back to the kids, flipped over on his back and swam circles around them upside down. The shore crowd cheered. As if taking a bow, the dolphin righted himself, swam between a youngster's legs then surfaced to loll on top of the water in the middle of the group to accept good-naturedly the children's hands that patted him in praise of his fine performance. The dolphin then lay on his back and lifted his tail high in the air and waved goodbye to the departing spectators who cheered and waved back.

I was struck by how much attention Boy paid to Lea, who was the eldest Holloway daughter. She spoke quietly to him and sometimes used hand signals that he appeared to understand perfectly. Lea told me later that she had been working with the dolphin by herself and was amazed at how quickly he learned.

After I photographed the family playing with the dolphin I relied on short letters from George to keep me up on the dolphin's activities.

Later I learned that Lea continued working with Boy in the early morning hours. She could be with him for a couple hours even on workdays. On the weekends she and Boy spent a lot of time together. The dolphin was learning by leaps and bounds. Sometimes she pushed her inflatable boat in the water and sped out the pass with Boy hot in pursuit. Once there she would beach the boat and the two of them would frolic around in the ocean, both of them getting to know each other better.

The difficult time was in the springtime when lots of fishermen buzzed the bay in their powerboats. All that activity was almost too much for the dolphin. It certainly was for the fishermen. A lot of hot words were fired at the dolphin for his bumping of their boats. Soon his actions became a problem.

The fishermen were very annoyed. The people who made money off these visitors began talking about what they should do about the dolphin. Almost everyone heartily disapproved of any thought of someone trying to remove *their* dolphin. After all, they argued, he was *their* dolphin by choice. He made it perfectly clear that he preferred the company of people to those of his own kind. "Leave him alone!" they insisted. And they meant it.

But there seemed no way for peaceful coexistence between the boaters and the dolphin. As the furor grew, so too did the dolphin's problems. More than once the dolphin felt the wrath of irate fishermen when his friendly bump against their boat brought him a most unfriendly bump of their oar against his dome.

Soon, the dolphin's once smooth brow began to show the scrapes and scars of these encounters. But no one was really sure which were battle scars and which the result of his fascination with whirling propellers. Only once was there absolutely no doubt what had happened. Someone speared the dolphin.

The Inlet's entire community lead by the Holloway family was up in arms when they learned about that. Lea immediately consulted a veterinarian and saw to it that the proper medications were administered to help heal the wound. It was such a shocking, unthinkable cruelty everyone knew that none of them would have ever done such a thing. Some outsider was to blame. Maybe some crazy Yankee mistook him for a shark. You heard all kinds of theories. Fortunately, the wound was superficial and soon healed. But from then on, the dolphin wore the unmistakable marks of a five-pronged fish spear on his flank. Such malice was more than anyone could understand. The only one who seemed to bear no bitterness over that unfortunate encounter was the dolphin himself.

Soon, newspapers carried accounts of the wild dolphin that had befriended the people of Forb's Inlet. As the dolphin's popularity grew, more people came to see him. Even people from the adjacent states of Georgia and Alabama made special trips to this small Florida fishing community to pay their respects to the friendly dolphin.

As his fame spread, it eventually attracted the attention of a commercial oceanarium that kept and trained dolphins for public performances. These businessmen felt that the dolphin would be a natural attraction for their dolphin show. They came to Forb's Inlet to see if this talented creature could be persuaded to go professional by joining the ranks of other captive dolphins that daily entertained crowds of people in exchange for free room and board.

For the first time the people of Forb's Inlet – both the pro-dolphin and the anti-dolphin people agreed on one thing – **no one**, they vowed, would ever take their dolphin away from them and turn him into a circus performer people had to pay to see. Their dolphin was born free, lived free and that's the way they intended to keep it.

Once or twice it seemed that some litigation might arise over the issue of who owned the wild dolphin and who had the right to claim him. But finally the dolphin lovers of Forb's Inlet settled the issue through mutual agreement. The dolphin was free to come and go but in the meantime Larry McGreggor, the owner of McGreggor's Boat Livery was given permission by the local council to keep the dolphin within his docks during the spring period when boat rentals were at their peak. Of course the dolphin would get free room and board and could still put on public performances for free whenever they visited him at the McGreggor's docks.

The Holloways did everything in their power to prevent this situation but the law was on the side of the people who were making a living off of the visiting tourists. Since the dolphin could leave the docks any time he chose, they considered him still free.

One weekend I drove down to the inlet to see what was happening. When I saw the dolphin, I knew things had changed. McGreggor the boat rental operator now kept the dolphin in an enclosure bounded by docks. It was a kind of pen about thirty feet square. All that really confined the dolphin in that shallow water was a chicken-wire fence strung around the dock pilings. The dolphin could easily leap over the low dock and escape whenever he wished. But apparently he chose not to do so. He had only been there a week but he seemed to have lost all interest in everything.

McGreggor had no idea what was wrong with him. He told me he never performed any more. The boat rental people saw that he had plenty of fresh mullet to eat but he seemed to have lost his appetite. He just stayed inside the enclosure. Surely, the fishermen had no complaints about this arrangement.

With other visitors, I walked out on the dock to see the dolphin. Instead of swimming around inside his pen as I had expected, the dolphin stayed away from the sides, remaining more in the middle of the enclosure, warily eyeing the people on the dock. Some children splashed water, trying to coax him closer so they could pet him. But the dolphin kept his distance, periodically lifting his head to breathe while watching the onlookers.

Only once did I see him respond to a spectator. An older boy tossed several pebbles toward him to attract his attention. The dolphin responded by lifting his head and squirting a sizable stream of water straight at his tormentor, scoring a direct hit. Everyone but the boy laughed. Then the crowd quickly dispersed. Most took it to mean that the dolphin was simply in no mood to play.

After the spectators left, I stood on the dock watching the dolphin. I felt depressed. It was not a happy scene. I had enjoyed seeing the dolphin happy, playing with and frolicking with children in the water. Not like this. Seeing him there by himself in the muddy water of his chicken-wire pen was just wrong, even if he could leap out of his pen. He apparently really didn't want to.

He looked totally dispirited. I wondered what had happened to cause that. Perhaps it was only my imagination, but at that moment I had the distinct impression that the dolphin's perpetual smile was no longer there.

I never saw the dolphin again after that. George later sent me a short note. All it said was, "We lost Nudgy last night."

When I read that I expected the worst had happened. I was sad that it had happened that way. I remembered him as being such a happy fellow. What had changed?

A couple years later when I was diving and photographing a project involving one of the two naval research towers off Panama City, I mentioned the dolphin to a naval officer. He just smiled at me. He was one of the sharp young naval scientists involved in that project. With a grin he said,

"I know what happened to that dolphin because I just married the woman he loved more than life itself. Her name is Lea."

# I You Home All Together

Once the McGreggors began keeping the dolphin at their docks, Lea appealed to everyone she could on how this was too cruel to imagine for a wild dolphin that had always been so free. The fact that he could get away if he wanted to also distressed Lea but she didn't dare go see him penned up that way. It would have been too painful for both of them. She didn't know how she would react. She just could not stand to see Boy like that.

Boy in turn did not understand why Lea had not come to get him; why she had not even visited him. The more he thought about it the more he lost interest in anything anymore. He even considered ending it for himself. This was not uncommon among dolphins. They simply took a last breath of air, sank to the bottom and no longer breathed again. But Boy would wait. He felt sure that Lea would come for him. But now it had been over a week. He ate little. He had no desire to eat. He was losing his strength fast. Boy was slowly dying.

When Lea felt that she had exhausted all the possibilities of freeing Boy, she knew there was no way. Whatever was to be done had to happen soon because she heard how poorly Boy was. That made up her mind.

Early the next morning, an hour before daylight she put her snorkeling gear into her inflatable along with the silver cover and pushed her boat into the water. The 15-horse Evinrude started at a touch and at low throttle simply purred the Cadet along the quiet bay toward the McGreggor docks. The moon was in and out of the clouds but at that hour no one was ever upset hearing a motor in the night. Too many were out doing things like crabbing or floundering right up until dawn.

But to make the white inflatable less obvious she pulled the silver boat cover over it after she dropped anchor and slipped into the water with her mask, fins and snorkel.

Swiftly she finned to the dock with its pilings wrapped in chicken wire. The dolphin felt the disturbance in the water. He scanned and knew who it was instantly. His heart surged!

In the darkness beyond the chicken-wire enclosure she heard him break the surface of the water.

"*Layyy-ahhh!*" he said softly.

Her heart leaped. "*Boy!*" she whispered.

Then he was at the fence, pushing against it with his head.

"No, Boy!"

He lifted his head out of water and looked at her. She gave him a hand signal for *Boy jump.*

He swiftly backed up and almost before she knew it she felt the movement of water as he surged forward and easily cleared the dock; his body hurtling over her head. Then she finned quickly to her boat.

She slipped over the side, pushed off the canvas, pulled her anchor and moments later the two of them were going full throttle down the bay. Boy was beside himself with joy. With the dolphin once again spinning in the wake of her small boat the two of them raced for the mouth of the inlet. Together they shot through it and out into the open Gulf of Mexico just as the golden orb of the sun rose over the eastern horizon.

But by then the inflatable was empty because Lea and Boy were in the water embracing each other, then racing around in circles together with each of them making the kinds of sounds only happy people and dolphins can make.

This kind of merriment wasn't long in attracting attention. It came in the form of six other dolphins that appeared out of no-where, acting as if they wanted to join the fun.

The entire group was busily clicking Dolphinese at each other and Lea saw that Boy was overjoyed to see them. He came up and she saw his eyes and knew he was himself again. She embraced him. She said, "Boy, go home," stretching her arms wide signing his Gulf home.

He responded, "Boy, go home Lea."

"No, Boy." She kissed him on his chin and pointed out to sea.

He looked at her and did the rapid head dipping yes motion as he fired off Buster's "Yap, yap, yap" laughter, then he turned on his back and did the tail waving in the air act that always ended his performances and drew so much applause from the watching crowd.

"**Yes, yes**!" shouted Lea," laughing too now as tears rolled down her cheeks. She clapped her hands knowing that he understood that meaning.

*"Good, Boy. Good."*

Lea watched the cavorting dolphins as they moved off leaping and rolling together until the happy group disappeared into the gradually brightening deep green color of the Gulf of Mexico. Then she started her boat, turned around and slowly headed back. She was crying but she was so happy for him.

After I heard this story from Lea's husband I sent Lea a belated wedding gift – a framed enlarged photograph I had taken of her whole family playing with their grinning friend, Boy.

On the back of her thank you note she wrote this:

"The following spring I was swimming off Sandy Point when Boy returned. We were so glad to see each other again. He still remembered everything I taught him. With him was a shy female dolphin. She was very pregnant. I could tell that Boy was very proud of her. He said to me, 'More Boy.'

"I said, 'Yes. Yes. Good, Boy.'

"Before we parted, he said, 'I you home all together, Laayyyy-ahhhh.'

"I clapped because that made me very happy," wrote Lea. "He told me that one day he would come to my home and our two families would be together again.

"I'm looking forward to that," she wrote, then added: "Thank you so much for your photograph of us all together when we were so happy playing with Boy. You have no idea how much that picture means to me.

Love, Lea Holloway."

# ADDENDUM

Over the years a number of scientists who have researched dolphin behavior believe that these mammals should be considered special. Since they possess unusually high intelligence compared to other animals means that dolphins should be considered non-human persons. They should have their own specific rights. It should be morally unacceptable anywhere in the world to keep them captive for entertainment purposes. And it especially should be forbidden to kill them intentionally for consumption or accidentally as a bycatch. To back up this outstanding proposal the countries that early on declared dolphins to be "non-human persons" are Chili, Costa Rica, Hungary, and India They all have banned the capture and import of live dolphins for entertainment. We hope that one day this proposal will be accepted worldwide. Any continued research on these remarkable mammals should be in the wild where they live free. As of 2020 here's how this proposal is progressing:

More than 2,100 dolphins and whales are being held in captivity at 343 facilities in 63 countries around the world, with the highest numbers of dolphinariums located in Japan (57), China (44), the United States (34), Russia (24), and Mexico (24), according to the Born Free Foundation.

This week, a vote on a California bill that would ban Orcas captivity was delayed by 18 months, pending an interim study. But, if it passes, California will join a growing list of U.S. states and localities and at least 14 countries that have outlawed the captive display of Orcas, dolphins, and in some cases, all wild animals.

Here are all the locales around the world that forbid the keeping of Orcas or dolphins in tanks for the amusement of paying customers.

**United States**

California

On Feb. 24, 2014, a proclamation declaring that all dolphins should have the right to freedom was passed by the Malibu City Council and subsequently signed by Mayor Joan House. "Whales and dolphins are known to be highly intelligent and emotional creatures," it declared, "and therefore deserve the right to their own freedom and lives."

On March 6, California state Assembly member Richard Bloom made international headlines by introducing the Orcas Welfare and Safety Act, which would make it illegal to "hold in captivity, or use, a wild-caught or captive-bred Orcas for performance or entertainment purposes." The bill would also ban captive breeding and artificial insemination of captive killer whales in California.

New York

State Sen. Greg Ball surprised anti-captivity activists by introducing a bill in February to ban "the possession and harboring of killer whales in aquariums and sea parks" in the state. On March 25, the Senate Standing Committee on Environmental Conservation voted in favor of the bill. New York has no captive Orcas, but animal welfare activists are nonetheless closely watching the symbolic measure.

South Carolina

In 1982, activist Mark Berman, now at the Earth Island Institute, home to Ric O'Barry's Dolphin Project, helped pass the first and only U.S. state law to ban marine mammals in captivity. In 2001, state officials amended the law, limiting protections to just cetaceans after Riverbanks Zoo in Columbia announced plans for a sea lion exhibit. "We will work very hard to defend the law if there's any attempt to change it further," Berman said in November 2013.


Hawaii

When a developer proposed in 2002 to construct a dolphinarium at a Maui shopping center, the Pacific Whale Foundation and other groups successfully lobbied the Maui County Council to ban the display of any captive whale or dolphins.


**Bolivia**

The Bolivian government made history in July 2009 by enacting the world's first ban on all animals in circuses and other public performance venues. The law was passed following an investigation by the U.K.'s Animal Defenders International, which found widespread abuse in Bolivian circuses, according to The Guardian.


**Chile**

Chilean law was amended in January 2005 to prohibit the

capture or import of any cetacean species, "for public exhibition or any other objective associated to its utilization by man."

## Costa Rica

The government of Costa Rica decreed new cetacean regulations in July 2005 making it "strictly forbidden" to catch and kill marine mammals, keep cetaceans and other marine mammals captive, or touch, feed, or trap any marine mammal.

## Croatia

In July 2009, Croatia's State Institute for Nature Protection enacted a regulation banning the keeping of cetaceans in captivity for commercial purposes. The only exemption would be for the rehabilitation and return of sick or injured animals to their natural environment.

## Cyprus

The nonprofit group Animal Responsibility Cyprus won a campaign to ban the importation of cetaceans in June 2011. The group says it was also successful in shutting down the Ayia Napa dolphinarium, the only one in the island nation, in 1999. "Subsequent applications to open captive dolphin shows were refused by the authorities," according to the ARC website. "In spite of Cyprus being a popular holiday spot, you will not see any so-called dolphinariums here."

## Greece

A campaign by Animal Defenders International and the

Greek Animal Welfare Fund prompted the Greek government to enact a ban in February 2012 on not only dolphin captivity but also the use of all animals in circuses. Greek law now forbids using animals in "recreational games, car racing platforms, musical concerts, exhibitions, fairs or other artistic or entertaining festivities." In January 2014, the law was overwhelmingly upheld by Parliament following a challenge by the Attica Zoological Park in Sparta.

## Hungary

This country's last dolphinarium was closed down and a ban on dolphin imports was imposed in 1992 after "one of the five illegally-imported dolphins from Ukraine died during the transfer, and another within a week of its arrival," according to the Armenian Weekly.

## India

On May 20, 2013, India's Ministry of Environment and Forests banned the keeping of captive dolphins for public entertainment. A statement from B.S. Bonal of the Central Zoo Authority declared that cetaceans do not in general survive well in captivity. "Confinement in captivity can seriously compromise the welfare and survival of all types of cetaceans by altering their behavior and causing extreme distress," he said. The ministry even declared that dolphins "should be seen as 'non-human persons' and as such should have their own specific rights."

## Nicaragua

On Feb. 2, 2003, Jorge Salazar Cardenal, then Nicaragua's

minister of the environment, confirmed in a letter to the World Society for the Protection of Animals that his country had "banned the use and exploitation of bottlenose dolphins indefinitely." Salazar added that the law "guarantees that in Nicaragua, these animals will be fully protected."

## Slovenia

According to WDC, Slovenian law "explicitly prohibits" the display of captive dolphins.

## Switzerland

The country's House of Representatives handed a major victory to captivity opponents when it outlawed the "keeping of dolphins in aquariums or for entertainment purposes" in March 2012. The Swiss Senate also banned the importation of dolphins. Meanwhile, the last two dolphins remaining in the country were sold to a facility in Jamaica in December 2013.

## Others

A few countries have standards so strict that it is nearly impossible to keep cetaceans in captivity, including Brazil, Luxembourg, Nicaragua, Norway, and the United Kingdom, where the last dolphinarium was closed in 1993. No company has been able to open in the U.K. since then, "because imposed standards exceed the viability of establishing a dolphinarium in the country," according to the Born Free Foundation.

# ABOUT THE AUTHOR

Author Robert F. Burgess has been called a Renaissance author because his books about true adventures cover a wide spectrum of time and events. A veteran of World War II where he served with the 88th Blue Devil Division Ski Troops in northern Italy, he writes traditional books and short Kindle e-books about true Vietnam War action.

Burgess is no stranger to sharks, shipwrecks, Spanish treasure, friendly dolphins and underwater archaeology. He writes about these subjects in such a way that readers feel they are the ones experiencing the adventure. His words make you believe you are swimming with the dolphins or getting lost in an underwater cave; crossing the Swiss Alps at midnight on a motor-scooter; partying with Ernest Hemingway in Pamplona, or being sized up by a hungry bull shark. He knows what it is like to explore underwater caves or a long lost 1715 Spanish Galleon. Join him in these adventures on Amazon.com.

**Other Books by Robert F. Burgess Available at Amazon.com**

1. To Majorca With Love
2. Real Cliffhangers
3. Hemingway's Paris and Pamplona, Then and Now
4. Meeting Hemingway in Pamplona
5. Florida's Golden Galleons
6. Secret World Of The Sharks
7. Lone Wolf of the Wolfhounds
8. Secrets Of A Happy Hooker
9. Ghost Sniper
10. Return Of The Ghost Sniper
11. Revenge Of The Ghost Sniper
12. The Sweet Goodbye
13. Zapping The Zebra
14. Two For The Marquesas
15. Diving To Adventure
16. Sailing To Adventure
17. Find More Treasure
18. How They Escaped
19. Diving Into The Past
20. They Found Treasure
21. Fire, Ice And Inca Gold
22. Catch More Lobsters
23. Finding Sunken Treasure
24. 1715 Treasure
25. Tracking Treasure By Computer
26. One Night On Scarborough Pond
27. Sniper Up!
28. Charlie, You're Not Perfect
29. Rolling Thunder
30. Carlos Hathcock's Longest Mission
31. Mystery Snipers, CIA Wizardry, and Our Fight against Isis
32. Charlie Brown Sniper